LNAT Practice Papers

Volumes One & Two

UniAdmissions

ISBN 978-1-912557-51-6

Published by *RAR Medical Services Limited*
www.uniadmissions.co.uk
info@uniadmissions.co.uk
Tel: 0208 068 0438

LNAT Practice Papers

4 Full Papers & Solutions

Aiden Ang
Rohan Agarwal

UniAdmissions

About the Authors

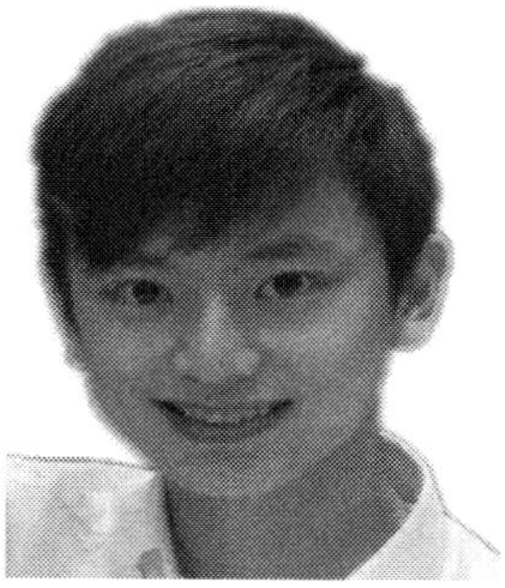

Aiden graduated from Peterhouse, Cambridge, with a First Class Honours Law degree and has tutored Oxbridge law applicants at *UniAdmissions* for two years.

Aiden scored in the **top 10% nationally in the LNAT** and is now a trainee solicitor at a top US firm in London. He has a keen interest in helping out students with application advice as he believes that students should get all the help they need in order to succeed in their applications. In his spare time, he likes to travel and run outdoors.

Rohan is the **Director of Operations** at *UniAdmissions* and is responsible for its technical and commercial arms. He graduated from Gonville and Caius College, Cambridge and is a fully qualified doctor. Over the last five years, he has tutored hundreds of successful Oxbridge and Medical applicants. He has also authored ten books on admissions tests and interviews.

Rohan has taught physiology to undergraduates and interviewed medical school applicants for Cambridge. He has published research on bone physiology and writes education articles for the Independent and Huffington Post. In his spare time, Rohan enjoys playing the piano and table tennis.

Introduction

The Basics

The Law National Aptitude Test (LNAT) is a 2 hour 15 minutes test that is split into two sections – Section A comprises 42 multiple choice questions based on several passages, and Section B consists of a selection of essay questions from which you will have to attempt one.

Many top law schools use the LNAT, including University of Oxford, University College London and King's College London, hence it is imperative to do well for this test in order to maximise your chances of securing a spot in a top law school.

The only way to improve your LNAT scores, especially in Section A, is to keep practicing and reviewing your answers and examination technique. Hence, we have compiled a few LNAT Mock Papers that have been meticulously written by our expert tutors, designed to resemble the actual test as much as possible.

There is a dearth of information available freely which understandably makes students nervous and unprepared for the test. Our Mock Papers come with expert solutions that aim to let you know where you've gone wrong and prepare you as much as possible for the actual test.

Preparing for the LNAT

Before going any further, it's important that you understand the optimal way to prepare for the LNAT. Rather than jumping straight into doing mock papers, it's essential that you start by understanding the components and the theory behind the LNAT by using a LNAT textbook. Once you've finished the non-timed practice questions, you can progress to using official LNAT papers. These are freely available online at **www.uniadmissions.co.uk/LNAT-past-papers** and serve as excellent practice. Finally, once you've exhausted past papers, move onto the mock papers in this book.

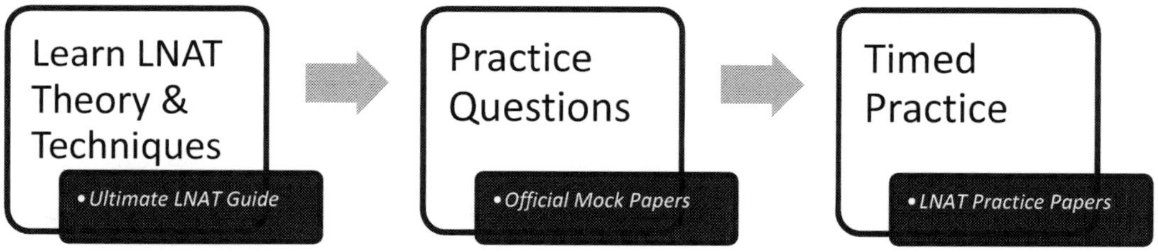

Already seen them all?

So, you've run out of past papers? Well hopefully that is where this book comes in. It contains four unique mock papers; each compiled by Oxbridge law tutors at *UniAdmissions* and available nowhere else.

Having successfully gained a place on their course of choice, our tutors are intimately familiar with the LNAT and its associated admission procedures. So, the novel questions presented to you here are of the correct style and difficulty to continue your revision and stretch you to meet the demands of the LNAT.

General Advice

Start Early

It is much easier to prepare if you practice little and often. Start your preparation well in advance; ideally ten weeks but at the latest within a month. This way you will have plenty of time to complete as many papers as you wish to feel comfortable and won't have to panic and cram just before the test, which is a much less effective and more stressful way to learn. In general, an early start will give you the opportunity to identify the complex issues and work at your own pace.

Prioritise

The MCQ section can be very time-pressured, and if you fail to answer the questions within the time limit you will be doing yourself a major disservice as every mark counts for this section. You need to be aware of how much time you're spending on each passage and allocate your time wisely. For example, since there are 42 questions in Section A, and you are given 95 minutes in total, you will ideally take about 130 seconds (just over two minutes) per question (including reading time for the passages) so that you will not run out of time and panic towards the end.

Positive Marking

There are no penalties for incorrect answers; you will gain one for each right answer and will not get one for each wrong or unanswered one. This provides you with the luxury that you can always guess should you absolutely be not able to figure out the right answer for a question or run behind time. Since each question in Section A provides you with 4 possible answers, you have a 25% chance of guessing correctly. Therefore, if you aren't sure (and are running short of time), then make an educated guess and move on. Before 'guessing' you should try to eliminate a couple of answers to increase your chances of getting the question correct. For example, if a question has 4 options and you manage to eliminate 2 options- your chances of getting the question increase from 25% to 50%!

Avoid losing easy marks on other questions because of poor exam technique. Similarly, if you have failed to finish the exam, take the last 10 seconds to guess the remaining questions to at least give yourself a chance of getting them right.

Practice

This is the best way of familiarising yourself with the style of questions and the timing for this section. Although the test does not demand any prior legal knowledge, you are unlikely to be familiar with the style of questions in all sections when you first encounter them. Therefore, you want to be comfortable at using this before you sit the test.

Practising questions will put you at ease and make you more comfortable with the exam. The more comfortable you are, the less you will panic on the test day and the more likely you are to score highly. Initially, work through the questions at your own pace, and spend time carefully reading the questions and looking at any additional data. When it becomes closer to the test, **make sure you practice the questions under exam conditions**.

Past Papers

Official mock papers are freely available online at **www.uniadmissions.co.uk/lnat-past-papers**. Practice makes perfect, and the more you practice the questions, especially for Section A, the better you will get. Do not worry if you make plenty of mistakes at the start, the best way to learn is to understand why you have made certain mistakes and to not commit them again in the future!

Repeat Questions

When checking through answers, pay particular attention to questions you have got wrong. If there is a worked answer, look through that carefully until you feel confident that you understand the reasoning, and then repeat the question without help to check that you can do it. If only the answer is given, have another look at the question and try to work out why that answer is correct. This is the best way to learn from your mistakes, and means you are less likely to make similar mistakes when it comes to the test. The same applies for questions which you were unsure of and made an educated guess which was correct, even if you got it right. When working through this book, **make sure you highlight any questions you are unsure of**, this means you know to spend more time looking over them once marked.

No Dictionaries

The LNAT requires a strong command of the English language, especially for Section B where you are asked to write an essay in 40 minutes. You are not allowed to use spell check or a dictionary, hence you should ensure that you written English is up to standard and you should ideally make close to no grammatical or spelling errors for your essay.

Section A might also contain several passages that might be quite dense to the ordinary reader, but the LNAT is aimed at testing a student's reading comprehension skills. If there is a word you are unsure about, most of them time you should be able to deduce the meaning based on the context of the passage.

Top tip! In general, universities tend to focus more on Section A of the LNAT in short listing candidate Section B tends to be more subjective, and may be used simply as a tiebreaker at times.

Keywords

If you're stuck on a question, sometimes you can simply quickly scan the passage for any keywords that match the questions. For example, by searching for 'old' in the passage or words related to 'old', it will help you to answer the question.

A word on timing...

"If you had all day to do your exam, you would get 100%. But you don't."
Whilst this isn't completely true, it illustrates a very important point. Once you've practiced and know how to answer the questions, the clock is your biggest enemy. This seemingly obvious statement has one very important consequence. **The way to improve your score is to improve your speed.** There is no magic bullet. But there are a great number of techniques that, with practice, will give you significant time gains, allowing you to answer more questions and score more marks.

Timing is tight throughout – **mastering timing is the first key to success**. Some candidates choose to work as quickly as possible to save up time at the end to check back, but this is generally not the best way to do it. Often questions can have a lot of information in them – each time you start answering a question it takes time to get familiar with the instructions and information. By splitting the question into two sessions (the first run-through and the return-to-check) you double the amount of time you spend on familiarising yourself with the data, as you have to do it twice instead of only once. This costs valuable time. In addition, candidates who do check back may spend 2–3 minutes doing so and yet not make any actual changes. Whilst this can be reassuring, it is a false reassurance as it is unlikely to have a significant effect on your actual score. Therefore, it is usually best to pace yourself very steadily, aiming to spend the same amount of time on each question and finish the final question in a section just as time runs out. This reduces the time spent on re-familiarising with questions and maximises the time spent on the first attempt, gaining more marks.

It is essential that you don't get stuck with the hardest questions – no doubt there will be some. In the time spent answering only one of these you may miss out on answering three easier questions. If a question is taking too long, choose a sensible answer and move on. Never see this as giving up or in any way failing, rather it is the smart way to approach a test with a tight time limit. With practice and discipline, you can get very good at this and learn to maximise your efficiency. It is not about being a hero and aiming for full marks – this is almost impossible and very much unnecessary (even Oxford will regard any score higher than 30 out of 42 as exceptional). It is about maximising your efficiency and gaining the maximum possible number of marks within the time you have.

Manage your Time:

It is highly likely that you will be juggling your revision alongside your normal school studies. Whilst it is tempting to put your A-levels on the back burner falling behind in your school subjects is not a good idea, don't forget that to meet the conditions of your offer should you get one you will need at least one A*. So, time management is key!

Make sure you set aside a dedicated 90 minutes (and much more closer to the exam) to commit to your revision each day. The key here is not to sacrifice too many of your extracurricular activities, everybody needs some down time, but instead to be efficient. Take a look at our list of top tips for increasing revision efficiency below:

1. Create a comfortable work station
2. Declutter and stay tidy
3. Treat yourself to some nice stationery
4. See if music works for you → if not, find somewhere peaceful and quiet to work
5. Turn off your mobile or at least put it into silent mode; silence social media alerts
6. Keep the TV off and out of sight
7. Stay organised with to do lists and revision timetables – more importantly, stick to them!
8. Keep to your set study times and don't bite off more than you can chew
9. Study while you're commuting
10. Adopt a positive mental attitude and get into a routine
11. Consider forming a study group to focus on the harder exam concepts
12. Plan rest and reward days into your timetable – these are excellent incentive for you to stay on track with your study plans!

Use the Options:

Some passages may try to trick you by providing a lot of unnecessary information. When presented with long passages that are seemingly hard to understand, it's essential you look at the answer options so you can focus your mind. This can allow you to reach the correct answer a lot more quickly. Consider the example below:

What, then, is it that gives to Sanskrit its claim on our attention, and its supreme importance in the eyes of the historian? First of all, its antiquity—for we know Sanskrit at an earlier period than Greek. But what is far more important than its merely chronological antiquity is the antique state of preservation in which that Aryan language has been handed down to us. The world had known Latin and Greek for centuries, and it was felt, no doubt, that there was some kind of similarity between the two. But how was that similarity to be explained? Sometimes Latin was supposed to give the key to the formation of a Greek word, sometimes Greek seemed to betray the secret of the origin of a Latin word. Afterward, when the ancient Teutonic languages, such as Gothic and Anglo-Saxon, and the ancient Celtic and Slavonic languages too, came to be studied, no one could help seeing a certain family likeness among them all. But how such a likeness between these languages came to be, and how, what is far more difficult to explain, such striking differences too between these languages came to be, remained a mystery, and gave rise to the most gratuitous theories, most of them, as you know, devoid of all scientific foundation. As soon, however, as Sanskrit stepped into the midst of these languages, there came light and warmth and mutual recognition. They all ceased to be strangers, and each fell of its own accord into its right place. Sanskrit was the eldest sister of them all, and could tell of many things which the other members of the family had quite forgotten. Still, the other languages too had each their own tale to tell; and it is out of all their tales together that a chapter in the human mind has been put together which, in some respects, is more important to us than any of the other chapters, the Jewish, the Greek, the Latin, or the Saxon. The process by which that ancient chapter of history was recovered is very simple. Take the words which occur in the same form and with the same meaning in all the seven branches of the Aryan family, and you have in them the most genuine and trustworthy records in which to read the thoughts of our true ancestors, before they had become Hindus, or Persians, or Greeks, or Romans, or Celts, or Teutons, or Slaves. Of course, some of these ancient charters may have been lost in one or other of these seven branches of the Aryan family, but even then, if they are found in six, or five, or four, or three, or even two only of its original branches, the probability remains, unless we can prove a later historical contact between these languages, that these words existed before the great Aryan Separation. If we find agni, meaning fire, in Sanskrit, and ignis, meaning fire, in Latin, we may safely conclude that fire was known to the undivided Aryans, even if no trace of the same name of fire occurred anywhere else. And why? Because there is no indication that Latin remained longer united with Sanskrit than any of the other Aryan languages, or that Latin could have borrowed such a word from Sanskrit, after these two languages had once become distinct. We have, however, the Lithuanian ugnìs, and the Scottish ingle, to show that the Slavonic and possibly the Teutonic languages also, knew the same word for fire, though they replaced it in time by other words. Words, like all other things, will die, and why they should live on in one soil and wither away and perish in another, is not always easy to say. What has become of ignis, for instance, in all the Romance languages? It has withered away and perished, probably because, after losing its final unaccentuated syllable, it became awkward to pronounce; and another word, focus, which in Latin meant fireplace, hearth, altar, has taken its place.

This is an extremely dense passage with a lot of information. **Looking at the options first makes it obvious that certain information are redundant** and allows you to quickly zoom in on certain keywords you should pick up on in order to answer the questions.

In other cases, **you may actually be able to solve the question without having to read the passage over and over again**. For example:

Which language does the writer state is the oldest?
A. Sanskrit B. Greek C. Latin D. Gothic E. Anglo-Saxon

If you read the passage first before looking at the question, you might have forgotten what the passage mentioned about which language was the oldest, and you will have to spend extra time going back to the passage to re-read it again.

You can save a lot of time by looking at the questions first before reading the passage. After looking at the question, you will know at the back of your head to look out for which language was stated as the oldest by the author, and this will save a considerable amount of time.

Keep Fit & Eat Well:

'A car won't work if you fill it with the wrong fuel' - your body is exactly the same. You cannot hope to perform unless you remain fit and well. The best way to do this is not underestimate the importance of healthy eating. Beige, starchy foods will make you sluggish; instead start the day with a hearty breakfast like porridge. Aim for the recommended 'five a day' intake of fruit/veg and stock up on the oily fish or blueberries – the so called "super foods".

When hitting the books, it's essential to keep your brain hydrated. If you get dehydrated you'll find yourself lethargic and possibly developing a headache, neither of which will do any favours for your revision. Invest in a good water bottle that you know the total volume of and keep sipping throughout the day. Don't forget that the amount of water you should be aiming to drink varies depending on your mass, so calculate your own personal recommended intake as follows: 30 ml per kg per day.

It is well known that exercise boosts your wellbeing and instils a sense of discipline. All of which will reflect well in your revision. It's well worth devoting half an hour a day to some exercise, get your heart rate up, break a sweat, and get those endorphins flowing.

Sleep

It's no secret that when revising you need to keep well rested. Don't be tempted to stay up late revising as sleep actually plays an important part in consolidating long term memory. Instead aim for a minimum of seven hours good sleep each night, in a dark room without any glow from electronic appliances. Install flux (https://justgetflux.com) on your laptop to prevent your computer from disrupting your circadian rhythm. Aim to go to bed the same time each night and no hitting snooze on the alarm clock in the morning!

Revision Timetable

Still struggling to get organised? Then try filling in the example revision timetable below, remember to factor in enough time for short breaks, and stick to it! Remember to schedule in several breaks throughout the day and actually use them to do something you enjoy e.g. TV, reading, YouTube etc.

	8AM	10AM	12PM		4PM	6PM	8PM
MONDAY							
WEDNESDAY							
THURSDAY							
FRIDAY							
SATURDAY							
SUNDAY							
EXAMPLE DAY		School			Section	Essay	Dinner

Top tip: Ensure that you take a watch that can show you the time in seconds into the exam. This will allow you have a much more accurate idea of the time you're spending on a question. In general, if you've spent >180 seconds on a section 1 question – move on regardless of how close you think you are to solving it.

Getting the most out of Mock Papers

Mock exams can prove invaluable if tackled correctly. Not only do they encourage you to start revision earlier, they also allow you to **practice and perfect your revision technique**. They are often the best way of improving your knowledge base or reinforcing what you have learnt. Probably the best reason for attempting mock papers is to familiarise yourself with the exam conditions of the LNAT as they are particularly tough.

Start Revision Earlier

Thirty five percent of students agree that they procrastinate to a degree that is detrimental to their exam performance. This is partly explained by the fact that they often seem a long way in the future. In the scientific literature this is well recognised, Dr. Piers Steel, an expert on the field of motivation states that *'the further away an event is, the less impact it has on your decisions'*.

Mock exams are therefore a way of giving you a target to work towards and motivate you in the run up to the real thing – every time you do one treat it as the real deal! If you do well then it's a reassuring sign; if you do poorly then it will motivate you to work harder (and earlier!).

Practice and perfect revision techniques

In case you haven't realised already, revision is a skill all to itself, and can take some time to learn. For example, the most common revision techniques including **highlighting and/or re-reading are quite ineffective** ways of committing things to memory. Unless you are thinking critically about something you are much less likely to remember it or indeed understand it.

Mock exams, therefore allow you to test your revision strategies as you go along. Try spacing out your revision sessions so you have time to forget what you have learnt in-between. This may sound counterintuitive but the second time you remember it for longer. Try teaching another student what you have learnt; this forces you to structure the information in a logical way that may aid memory. Always try to question what you have learnt and appraise its validity. Not only does this aid memory but it is also a useful skill for the LNAT, Oxbridge interviews, and beyond.

Improve your knowledge

The act of applying what you have learnt reinforces that piece of knowledge. An essay question may ask you about a fairly simple topic, but if you have a deep understanding of it you are able to write a critical essay that stands out from the crowd. Essay questions in particular provide a lot of room for students who have done their research to stand out, hence you should always aim to improve your knowledge and apply it from time to time. As you go through the mocks or past papers take note of your performance and see if you consistently under-perform in specific areas, thus highlighting areas for future study.

Get familiar with exam conditions

Pressure can cause all sorts of trouble for even the most brilliant students. The LNAT is a particularly time pressured exam with high stakes – your future (without exaggerating) does depend on your result to a great extent. The real key to the LNAT is overcoming this pressure and remaining calm to allow you to think efficiently.

Mock exams are therefore an excellent opportunity to devise and perfect your own exam techniques to beat the pressure and meet the demands of the exam. **Don't treat mock exams like practice questions – it's imperative you do them under time conditions.**

Before using this Book

Do the ground work

- Understand the format of the LNAT – have a look at the LNAT website and familiarise yourself with it: www.lnat.ac.uk/test-format
- Improve your written English by practicing writing and reading frequently.
- Try to broaden your reading by learning about different topics that you are unfamiliar with as the essay topics can vary greatly.
- Learn how to understand a writer's viewpoint by reading news articles and having a go at summarising what the writer is arguing about.
- Be consistent – slot in regular LNAT practice sessions when you have pockets of free time.
- Engage in discussion sessions with your friends to give you more ideas about certain essay topics.
- Download the LNAT simulator and have a go at doing in online – the actual test is done on a computer so you will want to be familiar with the format – www.uniadmissions.co.uk/lnat-past-papers

Ease in gently

With the ground work laid, there's still no point in adopting exam conditions straight away. Instead invest in a beginner's guide to the LNAT, which will not only describe in detail the background and theory of the exam, but take you through section by section what is expected. *The Ultimate LNAT Guide* is the most popular LNAT textbook – you can get a free copy by flicking to the back of this book.

Questions are seldom repeated, so don't rote learn methods or facts. Instead, focus on applying prior knowledge to formulate your own approach. If you're really struggling and have to take a sneak peek at the answers, then practice thinking of alternative solutions, or arguments for essays. It is unlikely that your answer will be more elegant or succinct than the model answer, but it is still a good task for encouraging creativity with your thinking. Get used to thinking outside the box!

Accelerate and Intensify

Start adopting exam conditions after you've done the official mock papers. Remember that **time pressure makes the LNAT hard** – if you had as long as you wanted to sit the exam you would probably get 100%.

Doing all the mock papers in this book is a good target for your revision. Choose a paper and proceed with strict exam conditions. Take a short break and then mark your answers before reviewing your progress. For revision purposes, as you go along, keep track of those questions that you guess – these are equally as important to review as those you get wrong.

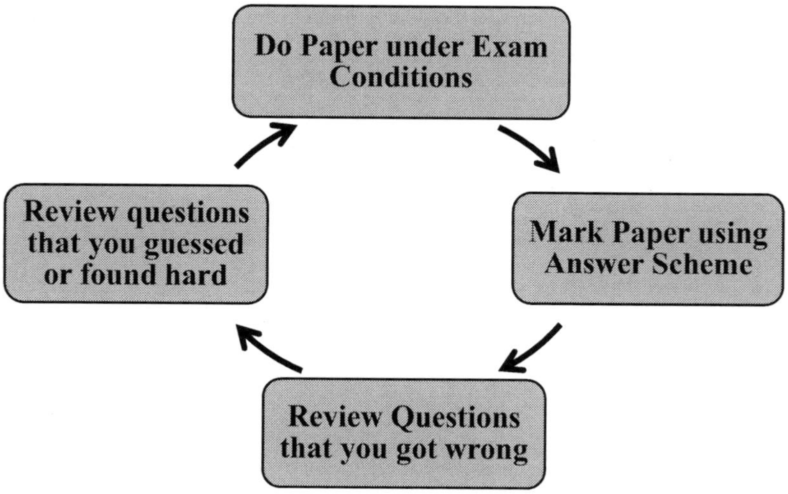

Once you've exhausted all the past papers, move on to tackling the unique mock papers in this book. In general, you should aim to complete mock papers every night in the seven days preceding your exam.

Section A: An Overview

What will you be tested on?	No. of Questions	Duration
Reading comprehension skills, deducing arguments, understanding certain literary tools, questioning assumptions	42 MCQs	95 Minutes

This is the first section of the LNAT, comprising several passages to read and a total of 42 MCQ questions. You have 95 minutes in total to complete the MCQ questions, including reading time for 10-12 passages. In order to keep within the time limit, you realistically have about two minutes per question as you have to factor in the reading time for the passages as well.

Not all the questions are of equal difficulty and so as you work through the past material it is certainly worth learning to recognise quickly which questions you should spend less time on in order to give yourself more time for the trickier questions.

Deducing arguments

Several MCQ questions will be aimed at testing your understand of the writer's argument. It is common to see questions asking you 'what is the writer's view?' or 'what is the writer trying to argue?'. This is arguably an important skill you will have to develop as a law student, and the LNAT is designed to test this ability. You have limited time to read the passage and understand the writer's argument, and the only way to improve your reading comprehension skill is to read several well-written news articles on a daily basis and think about them in a critical manner.

Assumptions

It is important to be able to identify the assumptions that a writer makes in the passage, as several questions might question your understand of what is assumed in the passage. For example, if a writer mentions that 'if all else remains the same, we can expect our economic growth to improve next year', you can identify an assumption being made here – the writer is clearly assuming that all external factors remain the same.

Fact vs. Opinion

It is important to be able to decipher whether the writer is stating a fact or an opinion – the distinction is usually rather subtle and you will have to decide whether the writer is giving his or her own personal opinion, or presenting something as a fact. Section A may contain questions that will test your ability to identify what is presented as a fact and what is presented as an opinion.

Fact	Opinion
'There are 7 billion people in this world…'	'I believe there are more than 7 billion people in this world…'
'She is an Australian…'	'She sounded like an Australian…'
'Trump is the current President…'	'Trump is a horrible President…'
'Vegetables contain a lot of fibre…'	'Vegetables are good for you…'

Section B: An Overview

What will you be tested on?	No. of Questions	Duration
Your ability to write an essay under timed conditions, your writing technique and your argumentative abilities	1 out of 3	40 Minutes

Section 2 is usually what students are more comfortable with – after all, many GCSE and A Level subjects require you to write essays within timed conditions. It does not require you to have any particular legal knowledge – the questions can be very broad and cover a wide range of topics.

Here are some of the topics that might appear in Section 2:

- Science
- Politics
- Religion
- Technology
- Ethics
- Morality
- Philosophy
- Education
- History
- Geopolitics

As you can see, this list is very broad and definitely non-exhaustive, and you do not get many choices to choose from (you have to write one essay out of three choices). Many students make the mistake of focusing too narrowly on one or two topics that they are comfortable with – this is a dangerous gamble and if you end up with three questions you are unfamiliar with, this is likely to negatively impact your score.

You should ideally focus on 3-4 topics to prepare from the LNAT, and you can pick and choose which topics from the list above are the ones you would be more interested in. Here are some suggestions:

Science

An essay that is related to science might relate to recent technological advancements and their implications, such as the rise of Bitcoin and the use of blockchain technology and artificial intelligence. This is interrelated to ethical and moral issues, hence you cannot merely just regurgitate what you know about artificial intelligence or blockchain technology. The examiners do not expect you to be an expert in an area of science – what they want to see is how you identify certain moral or ethical issues that might arise due to scientific advancements, and how do we resolve such conundrums as human beings.

Politics

Politics is undeniably always a hot topic and consequently a popular choice amongst students. The danger with writing a politics question is that some students get carried away and make their essay too one-sided or emotive – for example a student may chance upon an essay question related to Brexit and go on a long rant about why the referendum was a bad idea. You should always remember to answer the question and make sure your essay addresses the exact question asked – do not get carried away and end up writing something irrelevant just because you have strong feelings about a certain topic.

Religion

Religion is always a thorny issue and essays on religion provide strong students with a good opportunity to stand out and display their maturity in thought. Questions can range from asking about your opinion with regards to banning the wearing of a headdress to whether children should be exposed to religious practices at a young age. Questions related to religion will require a student to be sensitive and measured in their answers and it is easy to trip up on such questions if a student is not careful.

Education

Education is perhaps always a relatable topic to students, and students can draw from their own experience with the education system in order to form their opinion and write good essays on such topics. Questions can range from whether university places should be reduced, to whether we should be focusing on learning the sciences as opposed to the arts.

Section B: Revision Guide

SCIENCE

Resource	What to read/do
1. Newspaper Articles	• The Guardian, The Times, The Economist, The Financial Times, The Telegraph, The New York Times, The Independent
2. A Levels/IB	• Look at the content of your science A Levels/IB if you are doing science subjects and critically analyse what are the potential moral/ethical implications • Use your A Levels/IB resources in order to seek out further readings – e.g. links to a scientific journal or blog commentary • Remember that for your LNAT essay you should not focus on the technical issues too much – think more about the ethical and moral issues
3. Online videos	• There are plenty of free resources online that provide interesting commentary on science and the moral and ethical conundrums that scientists face on a daily basis • E.g. Documentaries and specialist science channels on YouTube • National Geographic, Animal Planet etc. might also be good if you have access to them
4. Debates	• Having a discussion with your friends about topics related to science might also help you formulate some ideas • Attending debate sessions where the topic is related to science might also provide you with excellent arguments and counter-arguments • Some universities might also host information sessions for sixth form students – some might be relevant to ethical and moral issues in science
5. Museums	• Certain museums such as the Natural Science Museum might provide some interesting information that you might not have known about
6. Non-fiction books	• There are plenty of non-fiction books (non-technical ones) that might discuss moral and ethical issues about science in an easily digestible way

POLITICS

Resource	What to read/do
1. Newspaper Articles	• The Guardian, The Times, The Economist, The Financial Times, The Telegraph, The New York Times, The Independent
2. Television	• Parliamentary sessions • Prime Minister Questions • Political news
3. Online videos	• Documentaries • YouTube Channels
4. Lectures	• University introductory lectures • Sixth form information sessions
5. Debates	• Debates held in school • Joining a politics club
6. Podcasts	• Political podcasts • Listen to both sides to get a more rounded view (e.g. listening to both left and right wing podcasts)

RELIGION

Syllabus Point	What to read/do
2. **Non-fictio books**	• Read up about books that explain the origins and beliefs of different types o religion • E.g. Books that talk about the origins of Christianity, Islam or Buddhism, theolog books etc.
3. **Talking to religious leaders**	• Talking to religious leaders may be a good way of understanding differen religions more and being able to write an essay on religion with more maturity an nuance • Talking to people from different religious backgrounds may also be a good way o forming a more well-rounded opinion
4. **Online videos**	• Documentaries on religion • YouTube channels providing informative and educational videos on differer religions – e.g. history, background

EDUCATION

Syllabus Point	What to read/do
2. **A Levels/I**	• Draw inspiration from what you are studying in your A Levels or IB – do you feel like what you are studying is useful and relevant? E.g. Studying arts versus science • Compare the education you are receiving with your friends in different schools or different subjects
3. **Education exchange**	• If you have an opportunity to go on an educational exchange, this might be a good opportunity to compare and contrast different educational systems • E.g. the approach to education in Germany versus the UK
5. **Online vid**	• Documentaries • YouTube Channels

Top Tip: Although you aren't required to have extra knowledge for the LNAT essay, doing so will allov you to make your essay stand out from the crowd. However, you should first **prioritise perfecting you writing style rather than doing extra reading** as the former will have a greater impact on your mark.

How to use this Book

If you have done everything this book has described so far then you should be well equipped to meet the demands of the LNAT, and therefore **the mock papers in the rest of this book should ONLY be completed under exam conditions**. This means:

- Absolute silence – no TV or music
- Absolute focus – no distractions such as eating your dinner
- Strict time constraints – no pausing half way through
- No checking the answers as you go
- Give yourself a maximum of three minutes between sections – keep the pressure up
- Complete the entire paper before marking and mark harshly

This means setting aside 2 hours and 15 minutes to tackle the paper. Completing one mock paper every evening in the week running up to the exam is an ideal target.

- Return to mark your answers, but mark harshly if there's any ambiguity.
- Highlight any areas of concern and read up on the areas you felt you underperformed
- If you inadvertently learnt anything new by muddling through a question, go and tell somebody about it to reinforce what you've discovered.

Finally relax… the LNAT is an exhausting exam, concentrating so hard continually for two hours will take its toll. So, being able to relax and switch off is essential to keep yourself sharp for exam day! Make sure you inish marking yc

Learn LNAT Theory & Techn [redacted] nate LNATGuide

Practice Questions [redacted] • Official Mock Pap

Timed Practice [redacted] • LNAT Practice Papers

Top Tip! You can get free copies of *The Ultimate LNAT Guide* and *LNAT Past Paper Worked Solu* [redacted] books by flicking to the back of this book.

Scoring Tables

Use these to keep a record of your scores from past papers – you can then easily see which paper you should attempt next (always the one with the lowest score).

[redacted]	[redacted]
Mock Pape	

You will not be able to give yourself a score for Section 2 per se as an essay is always marked rather subjectively – the best way to gauge your performance for Section 2 will be to compare your arguments and counter-arguments with the model answer, or get feedback from your teachers.

Top Tip! When repeating a mock paper, its best to attempt a different essay title to give yourself maxi [redacted] experience with the various styles of LNAT essays.

Mock Papers

Mock Paper A

1. Disc or Download: A Virtual Energy-Savings Debate

Adapted from 2014©. Copyright Environmental News Network

One of the best ways to spark an energy revolution is through the younger generation — and nothing quite speaks their language like video games.

But this issue has less to do with the content of these addictive games and more with how the younger generation consumes them.

Fantasy and adventure, sci-fi and first-person shooters, strategy and racing — video games today come in all types of genres with thousands of add-ons and customizable features to make each story a virtual reality. And with all of these choices comes two more: buy a copy of the video game on a disc or download the video game straight from the console?

At the crossroads of the decision lies Sony, one of the leading manufacturers of video games including the PlayStation® console. Sony offers the choice between direct download through an Internet connection and purchasing via game stores a Blu-ray copy of the game.

Now, one would think the former option is friendlier on the environment — no carbon footprint from shipping or driving to stores. However, cartridge collectors everywhere are about to rejoice. According to the *Journal of Industrial Ecology*, downloading a game from an Internet server can create a larger carbon footprint than driving to a store to purchase the game on Blu-ray disc.

A study was conducted by the *Journal of Industrial Ecology*, and although the report was based on a series of assumptions, the results were as follows:

"The CF [carbon footprint] of the life cycle of a downloaded 8.80 GB game amounted to 21.9 to 27.5 kg CO_2-eq (for lower and upper bounds of Internet energy intensity), whereas the result for a BD [Blu-ray disc] game was 20.8 kg CO_2-eq. Gameplay (use phase) accounted for 19.5 kg CO_2-eq emissions in both scenarios."

As observed, the carbon footprint from driving to the store and purchasing a Blu-ray disc is less comparatively, but there are some caveats. There is a threshold of 1.3 gigabytes, under which PlayStation® games are still more efficient to download. PlayStation® games are only getting larger, though.

According to the *Journal of Industrial Ecology*, game files have doubled in size between 2010 and 2013, and have increased by 25 percent from PlayStation 3 to PlayStation 4.

In fact, the advantage of discs is their ability to store massive amounts of data, which allows them to become exponentially better than direct downloads as their GB capacity increases. All that's needed is a little more transparency for all video games to be rated "E" — no, not "E" for everyone, but "E" for efficient.

1. Why does the author compare '"E" for everyone' and '"E" for efficient?
A. To illustrate the importance of efficiency
B. To use humour to emphasise the importance of universality
C. To bring together themes of environmentalism and gaming
D. To show that efficiency is not the main concern of video-game makers
E. To argue that the efficiency of video games should be more visible to consumers

2. Which of the following is an assumption that the author has made?
A. The younger generation will be more likely to engage in environmental debate if it surrounds a topic which interests them
B. That transparency regarding the efficiency of video games will encourage younger people to think more carefully about which games they purchase
C. That a higher carbon footprint is more detrimental for the environment
D. That a significant proportion of the younger generation have an interest in video games
E. Discs care better than downloads as they are capable of being shared amongst friends

3. Why does the author use a question as a conclusion to the third paragraph?
A. He wants the reader to engage in the debate through online comment
B. He implies that the issue of efficiency should be as important as the choice between different types of game
C. He wants to show that young people are overwhelmed by questions
D. He attempts to show that there is a real choice to be made between the two options, one which shouldn't be overlooked
E. He is trying to create an informal tone to the piece

2. Why Homework Matters

Adapted from 2014©. Edarticle

As an elementary/middle school teacher, I hear constant complaints about the issue of homework. There are valid points against overdoing it and even studies that suggest, in some cases, it doesn't always help. There's a big difference between busy work and assignments that are meaningful. Some researchers, like Sara Bennett and Nancy Kalish, propose that homework is a hidden cause of childhood obesity. Others, like Alfie Kohn, believe that the quality and quantity of assignments done at home should be addressed, pronto. So, why do students today still have to do this archaic activity?

- Although some teachers assign busy work, that is not always the case. Often times, the assignments students bring home are not only continuations of what was done in class, but are activities that help apply the knowledge learned earlier in the day.
- Some at-home assignments are enrichment activities that will nurture the creative side of children.
- It allows parents to see at firsthand what their child is doing in school, and gives them an opportunity to connect or communicate with their child on a different level, seeing where they stand academically.
- Even if it's studying or reviewing what was covered in class, it is an important reinforcement activity. This can eventually lead to information being stored into long-term memory.
- Research conducted by Harris Cooper (2006) suggests that students who complete homework tend to have higher scores on content related tests, than do students who have not completed content related homework.
- It can teach a child responsibility, which in turn will form into a good work ethic that will be useful for the rest of his/her life.
- Time management skills will develop and students will learn a valuable lesson about procrastination.
- It will allow students the opportunity to teach themselves, and learn how to manage schoolwork independently.

Although there is an ongoing debate about the merits and necessity of homework, the bottom line is that it doesn't look like it's going away any time soon. Sure, parents should question teachers and make sure that the homework is relevant and not going to last five hours, but the best possible action a student can take at the elementary age is to accept its inevitability. This will lead to time management strategies, allowing them to learn how to juggle a variety of activities on a daily basis, just like parents and all other adults do every day.

Studies at Duke University under Harris Cooper found a positive correlation between test scores and homework. "The results of such studies suggest that homework can improve students' scores on the class tests that come at the end of a topic. Students assigned homework in 2nd grade did better in mathematics, 3rd and 4th graders did better on English skills and vocabulary, 5th graders on social studies, 9th through 12th graders on American history, and 12th graders on Shakespeare." Of course, when it is overloaded, there's the case of diminishing returns.

Life in the working world is more competitive than ever before. Children need to learn the methods that will allow them to be successful in the life that's just ahead. Kohn suggests that homework doesn't help elementary school students, when research states otherwise. He is also a proponent of eliminating grades. Kohn's ideas generate excellent debate topics, but are not practical in a world that uses rankings for everything. So, even if you don't buy into the fact that homework will make a child a higher academic achiever in the short term (even though research states otherwise), realize that it just might create a human being with good habits, a rich work ethic, and success later on in the world outside academia.

4. Which of the following is a statement of fact rather than an assertion of opinion?
A. 'Children need to learn the method that will allow them to be more successful'
B. 'Kohn's ideas generate excellent debate'
C. 'Some researchers, like Sara Bennett and Nancy Kalish propose that homework is a hidden cause of childhood obesity'
D. 'There's a big difference between busy work and assignments that are meaningful'
E. 'it just might create a human being with good habits'

5. Which of the following does the author imply in the piece
A. Nurturing of a child's personality is equally as important as academic success
B. Good habits will help a child throughout his/her adult life
C. That s/he is fed up with hearing complaints about the issue of homework
D. Teachers who assign busy work are failing their students
E. Kohn's research is not trustworthy

6. What, according to the author, do children need to learn?
A. The methods to help them earn money in their later life
B. The mindset required in order to become successful in adulthood
C. To manage their schoolwork independently
D. Techniques that will help them to be successful
E. How to deal with an overload of homework

7. What is the main conclusion of the article?

A. Homework leads to good grades, which is important for children's prospects
B. Too much homework can be overwhelming for children
C. Homework is not helpful for academic achievement, but is instrumental in creating a rounded human being
D. Parents' opinions on how much homework their children have should be taken into consideration
E. Homework is likely to be helpful in a child's development, however important it ends up being from an academic perspective

3. What would independence mean for Scotland's racial minorities?

Adapted from 2014© Nasar Meer for the Guardian

Scotland's 'other' has firmly been the English. What happens when it starts to look more inward?

On Edinburgh's Royal Mile, the ancient road running from its 12th-century castle at the top down to the Enric Miralles-designed parliament at its bottom, you'll find some unlikely proponents of Scottish nationalism. Sporting tartan turbans and proudly brandishing the Saltire, the Sikh small-shop owners are sometimes viewed curiously by tourists and festival goers. The example is symbolic because at a time when Scottish identity is being appropriated in various arenas, it does raise the question of where ethnic and racial minorities fit into a country dominated by myths and legends of an ostensibly "white" nation dating back millennia.

Another way of putting this is to say that whatever else "Britishness" might be, we know that it's not the sole preserve of white Christians, but we're less sure about "Scottishness" (as we might be of "Englishness" if we looked close enough). Of course it depends where you go in Scotland, as it does in Britain as a whole, but surveys tell us that the Scots are no more exclusionary in their attitudes than the English.

With only around 2% ethnic minorities, however, it's a theory of tolerance that is yet to be tested and, as any student of nationalism will tell you, there's a fine line between inclusive and exclusive national identities. Until now though, and sectarian issues aside, it appears that Scotland's "other" has firmly been the English – what happens when it starts to look more inward?

Perhaps with the exception of Herman Rodrigues' 2006 exhibition on Scotland's Asian communities, little is said of the "new Scots". It is nevertheless a matter of enormous pride to the SNP that the only ethnic minority MSPs have been members of their party, the most recent being Humza Yousaf who earlier this month swore his oath of allegiance in Urdu, wearing traditional Pakistani clothes supplemented with a band of tartan. Elsewhere, less "visible" minorities, such as the Italians and now eastern Europeans, have stitched themselves into the fabric of Scotland's major cities, as indeed have Chinese groups and other east Asians. Hence one of Edinburgh's most beloved Scottish folk musicians is the Kirkcaldy-born Andy Chung.

Yet the most fascinating feature of Scottish nationalism is also the least noticed: there's a mighty difference between a nation's identity and people's national identities, which reveals itself in the saying that while England owned the British empire, it was the Scots who ran it. No wonder then that the Indian military has a Scottish tartan in its formal regalia (3rd battalion, the Sikh Regiment, traces its lineage from "Rattray's Sikhs" named after Captain Thomas Rattray of the 64th Regiment of Bengal Infantry). Whatever else people in Scotland think makes up their idea of Scottishness, the identity of Scotland as a historical nation cannot really be understood apart from that of India and other places of empire.

8. Why does the author use the example of Sikh shop owners selling Scottish paraphernalia?
A. To help explain the idea the concept of 'unlikely proponents of Scottish nationalism'
B. To raise the question of where ethnic and racial minorities fit into a historically 'white' country
C. To emphasise the concept that Scottish nationalism is not only for white Christians
D. To suggest that white Scottish people are intolerant of other ethnicities purporting to be Scottish nationalists
E. To ridicule the idea of multi-ethnic nationalism

9. What does the final paragraph of the extract conclude?
A. That there is a difference between people's individual national identities and the identities of a nation.
B. That a nation's identity and people within that country's national identity are entirely different concepts
C. The identity of Scotland is identical to those of other nations all around the world
D. That a nation's identity will have an effect on the national identities of individuals
E. That if Scotland loses the England as 'the other' it may turn inwards on its own minorities

10. All of the following are implied or stated in the piece except:
A. Scotland is becoming more multicultural
B. Scottish people are generally wary of their ethnic minorities
C. There has been very little writing done on ethnic minority Scots
D. Britain is established as a multicultural country
E. 'Englishness' as a concept is much less clear as a nationality than 'Britishness'

4. What price for honesty?

Adapted from 2014© Neil Reaich for BizEd

Pricing seems to be mentioned quite a lot in recent news headlines. The latest is the investigation by the Office of Fair Trading (OFT) into just how genuine the advertised price cuts in some large furniture stores really are. The OFT use the term 'reference pricing'. They've found cases in shops under investigation where not a single product had, in reality, been sold at the (supposedly original) higher price. The argument goes that since 95% of sales were at the lower or 'now' price then the stated original prices cannot really be genuine. Are we really so stupid as to be misled by reference pricing? When my wife buys some clothes in a sale and I ask how much it cost, she always responds by saying how much money she has saved. Well, unless she had the definite intention of buying it in the first place, she hasn't saved anything: in fact, she has spent it. The question is whether or not the reference pricing made a difference to her decision to buy the product. It must do, otherwise why is it so commonly used?

Heuristics suggests that people are not as rational as the standard economic model implies. Instead they use rules of the thumb, educated guesses or short cuts in decision-making. Anchoring refers to people making decisions based upon something they know to start with. For example, the anchor price of a jumper was £40 and there is 20 per cent discount offer making the new price £32 a saving of £8. If I decide to buy I might be thinking of the £8 saved because I didn't have to pay the full price, when I should be thinking logically about the actual price I am paying. In this case, there is too much focus on the anchor price, which is at such a level that I wouldn't have purchased the item anyway. In some cases, reference pricing is part of a strategy of price discrimination over time. Clothes shops attempt to capture consumer surplus by charging a high initial price for a few weeks for the 'must have and will pay' customers. The shops then give a discount which increases over time. New potential customers must now weigh up whether to buy now and get a 25 per cent discount or wait longer for a 5 percent saving and risk losing the deal because they have run out of their size.

Another tactic is to use time-limited offers where notice is given that the offer ends soon: buy now or miss out. Double glazing sales were notorious for using this tactic, encouraging customers to 'sign up today to get an extra 20 percent off'. Supermarkets are always giving volume offers, such as three for the price of two or get the second purchase for half the price. The supermarkets know we will pay more for the first item than we would for a second or third one. This tactic must lead to food waste as we are tempted to buy some products that we cannot possibly use before the sell-by date. The OFT also look at baiting sales where only a very limited number of products are available at the most discounted price. This sounds a little like discounts given for advanced booking train tickets. The OFT always makes mention of portioned 'drip' pricing where price increments drip through the buying process. It's those little add-ons that all add-up. Booking certain airline tickets comes to mind here. Restaurants often make an offer of a free second main course meal after buying one main course at full price. Now add on the fact that we may have full priced deserts, order drinks at a high mark up and then add the tip. Get your calculator out and the deal doesn't seem so good.

All these examples of price framing seek to alter a consumer's perception of the value of the offer. But there is more: have you purchased a printer at a ridiculously low price only to be stung on purchasing printer ink cartridges? Some businesses operate at a loss or low profit margin on certain items, to entice customers to part with more money on higher-profit goods. They bundle items together.

Some advice then:

- Use a calculator when shopping
- When buying clothes, divide the total by 50 to give you the average cost of wearing something once a week for a year: a shirt costing £25 will work out at 50 pence for every day worn;
- Avoid impulse buying on larger-ticket items;
- Only purchase multi-buys with long sell-by dates;
- Ignore the original price: it's only the current price you need to know about;
- Avoid limited-time offers.

11. What is the purpose of the inclusion of the phrase 'Booking *certain airlines* comes to mind here.'?

A. The author wants to leave the name of the airline open to individual inference, to make the statement as relevant as possible to all readers
B. The author wants to create a commonality between himself/herself and the reader, thereby making themselves more legitimate
C. The author wants to refer to a specific budget airline or group of airlines, but is fearful of naming one in particular
D. None of the above
E. All of the above

12. Which of the following is *not* a way that the author suggests retailers attempt to persuade customers into spending money on their products?

A. Stating that the 'original' price of an item is higher that it has ever really been sold, thereby creating the illusion of saving money
B. Splitting up the real cost of a product into a number of small, necessary, purchases
C. Raising the price of product - marketing as a 'luxury product' so that it will become more desirable
D. Giving some items for a reduced price if you buy in bulk
E. Slowly decreasing the price over time, creating a highly-pressured decision between buying now, or gambling that a product will be available at a cheaper price later

13. Why is it suggested that people are not as rational as the standard economic model implies?

A. To further the author's main point that people's decisions are influenced by different pricing models implemented by retailers
B. People make mistakes in their decision making - they aren't as thorough as they could be in the analytical process
C. To emphasise that the standard model is wrong, and that we must look beyond it to explain people's commercial behaviour
D. People are irrational, incapable of making decisions based on evidence
E. People are blind to price-based marketing

14. What is the overall purpose of the extract?

A. To advise consumers on how to make more rational decisions when shopping
B. To persuade retailers to be more honest in their pricing strategies
C. To warn consumers of the dangers of shopping without thinking about marketing
D. To inform readers about the different strategies utilised by retailers
E. To explore the concept of 'honest pricing' and come to a conclusion about the meaning of that term

5. A-level students: if you don't get into a Russell Group university, skip going altogether

Adapted from 2014© Christopher Giles for the Telegraph

There is little point getting into thousands of pounds of debt for a degree in 'Make-up and Hair Design', writes Christopher Giles.

Students who have received your A-level results, please listen up. If you have not – or do not – get into a top UK university, don't go at all. Results day is stressful. Euphoria. Relief. Disappointment. Frustration. Anxiety. It's emotional, but you'll be fine. Just follow my advice: if you aren't going to a Russell Group university or otherwise respected institution, forget about it altogether. Life is about making the right investments and university is pretty big one. It has to be worth every penny.

If, after the emotional roller coaster, you do decide to go to university, you are going to have a lot of debt. It is likely you'll owe £43,000, thanks to recent policies from the suits in Westminster. This will be money taken from your income for years to come (perhaps even for 30 years).

It is not just a financial investment. It is an investment of your time. If you live to 81, the average UK life expectancy, you would have spent 2.4 percent of your life at university. If this is 2.4 per cent of your life studying adventure sports, tourism or homeopathy, it probably won't propel your career. It is true that many have a love for academia – but if that's not you, don't be a sheep. Getting into and going to university used to be a big deal; now it's considered the norm. Don't let that fear of missing out sway you.

Time for some optimism: choosing not to go to university because you haven't got into one of the elite institutions shows good judgment. The appetite for mass university attendance is flagging. In fact, the stigma attached to having a weak degree could be worse than not having one at all. It is a nice sentiment to want everyone to go to university, but in reality it's not such a good idea.

To help you out, I've found some of the worst universities for graduate employability (via The Complete University Guide) and some strange courses to avoid. These universities really are the bottom of the pile and here is a selection of courses they offer, along with annual tuition fees.

The University of Sunderland: Fashion Product and Promotion (£7,800), Glass and Ceramics (£8,500), Sports Journalism (£8,500).

Southampton Solent University: Make-up and Hair Design, Football Studies, Cruise Industry Management. All of these courses cost £8,050.

The University of East London: Songwriting, Computer Game Design (Story Development), Hospitality and International Tourism Management. The University of East London ranks bottom in terms of graduate prospects in the UK and they charge £9,000 a year for full-time undergraduate courses.

Despite the huge debt, and wasted hours of your life, university does provide you with general life skills. Like the ability to work with a hangover, pay rent, and call your mum every weekend. Virtues these may be, but I am certain life experience isn't exclusive to university. It is just a costly way of getting it. Especially if what you're paying for is a tumbleweed degree that's going to float straight past employers.

The UK has some of the world's best universities. It also has quite a few average ones. So when you finally get through UCAS's 10,000-mile internet traffic jam, try to think with a cold rational mind: is it worth it?

15. What assumption does the author make in his discussion of university as 'an investment'?
A. Going to university will cost a significant amount of money
B. People will not be supported by family members in their financial commitment to pay university fees
C. Time spent at university is time wasted
D. Politicians do not have students' best interests at heart
E. There is no other reason why someone would choose to go to university except as an investment for the future

16. Which of the following is true according to the author?
A. University teaches people more than only the subject they study
B. A decision not to go to university is indicative of shrewdness
C. Since the rise in fees, university has become too expensive
D. A degree in 'Glass and Ceramics' is worthless
E. Only Oxbridge universities are worth attending

17. Which of the following is a possible description of the writer's opinion of the nature of the university system inferred from this passage?
A. Extortionate
B. Beneficial
C. Flawed
D. Worthless
E. Good value for money

6. Maria Miller: thank you and goodbye

Adapted from 2014© Simon Tait for 'The Stage' (edited)

She "has done an effective job in making the case for the value of public funding" Bazalgette says in response to the news that the arts are to get a ring-fenced 5% cut when ACE had been told to model for 10% and 15% scenarios for 2015/16.

But it is rather damning with faint praise. He goes on to say: "It is hugely encouraging that the Chancellor and the Treasury have listened to the argument that the arts and culture makes such a valuable contribution to our quality of life and the economy".

The argument made by the secretary of arts and culture, note, not the secretary of state.

DCMS (Department for Culture, Media and Sport) as a whole has got a less generous cut of 8%, and the deal for the arts appears to have been negotiated separately by the likes of Bazalgette and national museum directors like Nicholas Serota who, three weeks ago, went to George Osborne directly with economic arguments for a more lenient treatment of the sector. It was at this point that Osborne and the Treasury finally "got it" and realised how damaging a bigger arts cut would be to the economy, for negligible saving.

It means that Mrs. Miller cannot simply pass on to the arts the 8% cut as she and her predecessor, Jeremy Hunt, have done in the past because there is no fat in the DCMS, having been cut to the bone already, to absorb a new reduction itself. As it is, she will have to find the saving from elsewhere in her budget. Nevertheless, she has hung out and got a better settlement than most other government departments who are suffering at least 10% reductions as the government tries to find more savings, but it seems the knives are out not for culture or the arts but for Miller herself.

The knives appear to be out for her in government for a number of reasons, including not dealing decisively with Leveson. The culture secretary has also been the subject of unprecedented vilification in the Tory press, with the Daily Mail's drama critic Quentin Letts declaring a couple of weeks ago that "Culture is the department where a country can assert its character. If only its Secretary of State had one". In May, she made her first speech on the arts, calling for the economic argument to be made, Letts conceded, but "Where was the question of morality in Mrs. Miller's approach to the arts? Where was the vision that the arts can civilise us? Where was the idea of the arts as the most meritocratic of gifts, a route which can offer talented and aspiring youngsters a route to self-fulfillment…? There is not even much impression she is an arts lover. It was a speech that could have been given by any one of her departmental officials".

Her desperate attempts to grab a positive headline culminated last week in a damp squib of an announcement about the First World War centenary commemoration, in which nothing new was announced (except that 600-odd streets in England were to be renamed after VC winners from the Great War), and the major news about the cultural element cannot be revealed before August. On Friday, The Times's normally gentle columnist Richard Morrison wrote that "Some (culture secretaries) have been bores; some bluffers. But not one has depressed me as Maria Miller does.

As for the arts, the triumph is substantial and this might be a seachange in the way governments see the sector. The Arts Council, as fuel for the Bonfire of the Quangos, has taken an enormous battering since 2010 and the sector has correctly acknowledged that there is no case for "special treatment" while cuts amounting to 33% have been meted out, and of 50% to ACE itself. But now culture has established the principle that it is a special case after all, and with sense and imagination much of the effect of the new 5% cut might be ameliorated through the National Lottery.

The question now is whether that principle will be accepted by the other great subsidisers of the arts, the local authorities in whose hands the futures of dozens of theatres lie and whose extreme economic pain is even greater than Osborne's.

18. Which of these premises, if true, would most weaken the author's argument for the importance of funding for the arts?

A. Funding for the Emergency services is in decline and has been for years
B. The EU has recently passed legislation mandating that each country must increase state funding for the arts yearly in line with inflation
C. There is no evidence that the cost involved in increasing funding for the arts is justified by the eventual benefits
D. There is little evidence to suggest that funding for the arts would benefit a broad range of people
E. There is a correlation between increased funding for the arts and drop in the average GCSE grade

19. None of the following show the author's distaste for Maria Miller except:

A. 'not one has depressed me as Maria Miller does'
B. 'her desperate attempts to grab a positive headline'
C. 'it is rather damning with faint praise'
D. 'she has hung out and got a better settlement'
E. 'In May she made her first speech on the arts'

20. Which of the following is not stated in the extract?

A. The culture secretary now cannot pass cuts in budget straight onto the arts
B. Ms Miller is not universally accepted within government
C. The arts have had a better than expected outcome in relation to forecasts
D. The National Lottery's input will make up the whole of the 5% cut in the arts
E. Ms Miller announced a 'First World War centenary commemoration'

21. What, according to the author, is 'the question'?

A. Whether the idea that arts are more worthy than they once were is yet widely accepted
B. Whether the idea that arts are more worthy than they once were can be widely accepted
C. Whether the idea that arts are a 'special case' is correct given the many differing opinions
D. Whether the arts should be considered a 'special case'
E. Whether the idea that the arts should be treated differently will be reflected at a regional level

7. What makes a terrorist?

Adapted from 2014© Simon Allison for the Institute of Security Studies (edited)

Given the extent to which it dominates global news and politics, it is remarkable how little we know about the men – and, very occasionally, women – behind Islamic extremism. How are people drawn into such radical politics? What type of person becomes a terrorist? What is it that forces radicals out of day-to-day politics and into the extreme and often violent margins of society?

To discourage radicalisation we need a proper answer to the question of why and how people are radicalised. Anneli Botha, a senior researcher on terrorism at the Institute for Security Studies, asked members of radical groups themselves, specifically al-Shabaab and the Mombasa Republican Council.

Al-Shabaab is an Islamic extremist group that seeks principally to create an Islamic state in Somalia, although its ambitions and operations don't stop at the Somali border. The MRC, although often associated with al-Shabaab, is a distinct organisation with a very different agenda. It advocates for the secession of Kenya's coastal areas, and emphasises land grievances and economic and political marginalisation. It is a predominantly, but not exclusively, Muslim organisation.

95 interviews were conducted with individuals associated with al-Shabaab and 45 individuals associated with the MRC. Most of the respondents (96%) were male. From these interviews, Botha was able to observe patterns around their education, family background, religion and ethnicity as well as interrogate their motivations for joining and staying with radical groups.

There is no such thing as a typical extremist, however, it is possible to observe certain trends from the data. Almost all respondents grew up in a male-dominated household. Even when the father had passed away, usually a male relative stepped in to assume the patriarchal role. Over 70% of all respondents experienced corporal punishment at home, although most said that this wasn't too severe. Unexpectedly, around 60% of all respondents were middle children. "Middle children are known to experience the greatest sense of 'not belonging'," said Botha, explaining that this makes them especially vulnerable to close-knit radical groups, which can fill this void.

"When asked to clarify [what] finally pushed them over the edge, the majority of both al-Shabaab and MRC respondents referred to injustices at the hands of Kenyan security forces, specifically referring to 'collective punishment'," said Botha.

Respondents complained that "all Muslims are treated as terrorists" and that "government and security forces hate Islam". Some pointed to more specific examples, such as the assassination of Muslim clerics, or even particular incidents, such as an alleged assault by Kenyan police on a group of Muslims.

It is this last point that is most relevant for policymakers who are looking to contain the threat of extremism in Kenya. Simply put, a counter-terrorism strategy that relies on mass arrests, racial profiling and extrajudicial killings is counter-productive. These tactics have radicalised dozens, if not hundreds, of individuals, argues Botha, "ensuring a new wave of radicalism and collective resolve among their members, ultimately indicating that threats of violence or imprisonment are rarely effective deterrents."

Botha's research gives unprecedented insight into the background and motivations of the people who make up extremist organisations in Kenya. This is what a Kenyan radical looks like. Now it is up to Kenya's policymakers to tailor their responses accordingly.

22. According to the article, which of the following statements are accurate?
A. Extremists tend to share similar childhood experiences
B. Extremists are mostly male
C. Recent counter-terrorism strategies have led to increased radicalisation
D. All of the above
E. Both B and C

23. Based on the article, which of these pairs of ideas are not shown to be causally related?
A. Global coverage of radicalism and rise in extremism
B. Mass arrests and radicalism
C. Patriarchy and membership of extremist groups
D. An understanding of radicalisation and a reduction in radicalisation
E. Generalisation and frustration

24. What can be inferred from Botha's research as the definitive reason why most people become radicalised?
A. Patriarchal upbringing
B. Being a 'middle child'
C. Being overtly religious
D. None of the above
E. Impossible to say

25. Which of the following can be said to be the main conclusion of the final two paragraphs?
A. Radicalism is not always a result of indoctrination, background and childhood circumstances play a part too
B. The knowledge gained from this study about extremism in Kenya can be used to inform governments throughout the world
C. Policymakers should realise that most extremists identify unjust government activity as the ultimate reason why they became radicalised
D. Policymakers should take into consideration that the threat of extremism grows with an aggressive counter-terrorism policy
E. Policymakers should realise that extremism is best tackled with greater understanding of the reasons behind fanaticism

8. Drugs laws play 'cat and mouse' with creators of legal highs, says senior government adviser

Adapted from 2014© David Barrett for the Telegraph

Drug control legislation is being forced to play "cat and mouse" with the creators of an ever-expanding range of new "legal highs", the government's senior drug adviser has warned.

Professor Les Iversen, chairman of the Advisory Council on the Misuse of Drugs (ACMD), said the category of synthetic drugs – formally known as "novel psychoactive substances" – was growing all the time and legislation was struggling to keep up. He said the council, which advises the Home Secretary on classifying legal and illegal substances, had already reviewed the controls on legal highs in 2009 and 2012 before the launch of its current enquiry earlier this year.

"It looks as though we might have to go on doing this," he said. "It's a cat and mouse game but the cat should not withdraw in defeat."

Chemists who create synthetic drugs, such as mephedrone, to mimic the effects of illegal drugs like cocaine or heroin have been known to tweak the chemical composition of substances to stay one step ahead of the law. A European body which monitors new substances appearing on the black market said 80 different new types of legal high appeared last year.

Prof. Iversen added that the term "legal high" was now inappropriate because many of the substances, including mephedrone, have been made illegal. "The number of serious harms such as deaths emerging from this group of drugs is not all that staggering but it is an issue that we will certainly continue to consider," he said, adding that several announcements on the council's work in this area are due soon once they have secured ministerial approval.

The chairman also said during a meeting of the ACMD in central London that the growth of online pharmacies was leading to far wider abuse of prescription drugs which are legitimately available as painkillers or other types of medication.

"The misuse of medicines has become more of a topic because prescription medicines are so much more easily available on the internet," said the chairman, a retired Oxford University professor of pharmacology. "It's pretty easy to buy most medical products and this gives us a problem that is not easy to solve. We are going to try to evaluate the magnitude of the problem."

Prof. Ray Hill, chairman of the ACMD's technical committee, said it was currently looking at abuse of a drug called pregabalin which is used to alleviate pain and anxiety, and to treat epilepsy. "We are getting a variety of reports now from various parts of the UK that this drug is being misused," said Prof Hill.

"It's a drug that has some similar characteristics to opioid drugs when taken in very high doses. It's probably too soon to have substantive data on its harmful effects."
Prof. Iversen said: "The misuse of pregabalin is a surprise to all of us. This is a relatively new phenomenon and we're looking at how serious a problem this is."

26. Why is it suggested that the misuse of medicines is becoming more prevalent?
A. Growth of online pharmacies
B. Widespread use of the internet
C. The range of 'legal highs' is 'ever-expanding'
D. Legislation cannot keep up with chemists creating synthetic drugs
E. It is becoming easier to buy prescription drugs

27. Which of the following can be seen as being implied by Professor Iversen?
A. Legislators are giving up on the fight against legal highs
B. There is a labelling issue with so-called 'legal highs'
C. Pregabalin is being used more widely than before
D. The problem is becoming more difficult to deal with
E. The misuse of medicine is a longstanding issue

28. How many individuals are referred to in the extract?
A. 1
B. 2
C. 3
D. 4
E. 5

9. The world needs to talk about child euthanasia: Mercy for all?

Adapted from 2014© David Barrett for the New Scientist

EUTHANISING an infant is not technically difficult. Intravenous sedatives are used to silence the brain, followed by a pain medication such as morphine. This is often enough to trigger respiratory arrest and death, but if not, neuromuscular blockers are added, and the child dies. The process takes 5 to 10 minutes. Belgium has just become the first country to legislate in favour of child euthanasia at any age. However, there is a partial precedent. In 2005, the Netherlands recognised the Groningen protocol, a set of criteria outlining the circumstances under which ending the life of an infant under the age of 1 is permissible. Under those guidelines – which were written by Verhagen – euthanasia can only be undertaken if an infant's diagnosis and prognosis are certain and confirmed by an independent doctor, there is evidence of hopeless and unbearable suffering, both parents give their consent, the procedure follows medical standards, and all details are documented. Dutch children aged between 1 and 12 cannot be euthanised under any circumstances, although Verhagen and others are working to change that. While euthanasia remains technically illegal for infants in the Netherlands, doctors are not prosecuted so long as the protocol's criteria are met.

Opponents argued that this would lead to a slippery slope of infant euthanasia. The opposite happened. Since 2005, there have been only two cases in the Netherlands. Both involved babies with lethal epidermolysis bullosa, a disease of the connective tissues. This decline in euthanasia correlates with an increase in late-term abortions. Previously, most euthanasia cases involved babies born with severe to extreme spina bifida – a congenital disorder in which some of the vertebrae do not fully form. Doctors found that surgery was not possible and that the child would suffer constantly. In 2007, the Netherlands began offering free ultrasound scans at 20 weeks of pregnancy, at which point spina bifida can be detected. Mothers whose babies are diagnosed with the disease can then decide whether to terminate the pregnancy. This is not necessarily the best course for everyone in this situation. Only the most extreme cases of spina bifida are deemed hopeless, and it is impossible for doctors to precisely gauge the severity in utero. Having infant euthanasia as an option allows mothers to be sure that their baby has no chance of survival before ending its life. But, as Verhagen says, in practice most in this situation decide not to take any chances and terminate the pregnancy.

The means of ending a baby's life are subject to debate. Recently, the line between proactive palliative care – applying pain medications that may hasten death – and euthanasia has become more blurred. In some countries, including the US, food and fluid may be withdrawn in some circumstances. But palliative care practices do not necessarily result in a quick death for a terminally ill infant. Death by dehydration and starvation can take days or weeks and it is impossible to guarantee that the child – even heavily medicated – does not suffer. Moreover, no one doubts that death is the outcome of withholding life-sustaining care and support. Rather than draw out the inevitable, would it not be less cruel to swiftly end that life, alleviating all risk of unnecessary suffering? Belgium and the Netherlands have chosen to face this dilemma directly. Of course, not every country is as progressive, there will always be those who – due to religious or personal beliefs – oppose ending a human life. In the US, for example, reaching a federal consensus on the subject of infant euthanasia seems unlikely. On the other hand, progressive states such as Oregon might someday implement their own laws on it, much as they have for assisted suicide in adults. Whether this will ever come to pass remains to be seen. As Verhagen wrote in *The New England Journal of Medicine*, "This approach suits our legal and social culture, but it is unclear to what extent it would be transferable to other countries." For most parts of the world, a refusal to even discuss the subject dominates. As unpleasant as it is, parents, physicians, hospitals and nations need to confront this issue as a matter of responsibility towards both infants born into hopeless circumstances and their families.

29. What assumption does the author make in the last paragraph?
A. That late term abortion has recently become legalised
B. That fathers do not have a say in whether or not a child is to be aborted
C. It is a positive step that infant euthanasia has decreased in frequency
D. Epidermolysis Bullosa will always lead to early death
E. Mothers who terminate a pregnancy without being sure that their foetus' disease will be fatal are negligent

30. What is the main conclusion of the article?
A. Spina bifida is a horrific disease
B. Infant euthanasia should be widely legalised
C. Late term abortion can pre-empt a logical decision on the continuation of an infant's life
D. More of an agreement should be reached about the benefits of legalisation of child euthanasia in certain, narrow, circumstances
E. Infant euthanasia should be discussed more openly

31. Which of the following (if true) strengthens the author's argument?

A. Spina bifida's survival rate for newborns is 10%
B. Upon hearing about the inhumane palliative care treatment, 70% of parents with children with terminal, painful illness would choose euthanasia above practice palliative care options
C. Belgium's child mortality rate has risen by 25% since the legalisation
D. Spina bifida has been proven to cause continuous excruciating pain to infants from the moment of birth
E. The President of the European Union has given a speech suggesting that an investigation should be conducted into the possible benefits and problems of extending palliative care practices to cover child euthanasia

32. What is most likely to be the reason that the author begins the article with the sentence 'Euthanizing a child is not technically difficult.'?
A. Stating that euthanasia is not *technically* difficult implies that the real problems lies in its *emotional* difficulty
B. To grab the readers' attention at the beginning of the extract
C. To inform the reader about the methods used in infant euthanasia
D. None of the above
E. All of the above

10. Brazil releases 'good' mosquitoes to fight dengue fever

Adapted from 2014© Julia Carneiro for the BBC

The hope is they will breed, multiply and become the majority of mosquitoes, thus reducing cases of the disease.

The initiative is part of a programme also taking place in Australia, Vietnam and Indonesia.

The intracellular bacteria, Wolbachia, being introduced cannot be transmitted to humans.

The programme started in 2012 says Luciano Moreira of the Brazilian research institute Fiocruz, who is leading the project in Brazil. "Our teams performed weekly visits to the four neighbourhoods in Rio being targeted. Mosquitoes were analysed after collection in special traps. "Transparency and proper information for the households is a priority."

Ten thousand mosquitoes will be released each month for four months with the first release in Tubiacanga, in the north of Rio.

'Good' bacteria

The bacterium Wolbachia is found in 60% of insects. It acts like a vaccine for the mosquito which carries dengue, Aedes aegypti, stopping the dengue virus multiplying in its body.

Wolbachia also has an effect on reproduction. If a contaminated male fertilises the eggs of a female without the bacteria, these eggs do not turn into larvae. If the male and female are contaminated or if only the female has the bacteria, all future generations of mosquito will carry Wolbachia.

As a result, Aedes mosquitoes with Wolbachia become predominant without researchers having to constantly release more contaminated insects.

In Australia this happened within 10 weeks on average. The research on Wolbachia began at the University of Monash in Australia in 2008. The researchers allowed the mosquitoes to feed on their own arms for five years because of concerns at the time Wolbachia could infect humans and domestic animals.

Three more neighbourhoods will be targeted next, and large scale studies to evaluate the effect of the strategy are planned for 2016.

Dengue re-emerged in Brazil in 1981 after an absence of more than 20 years. Over the next 30 years, seven million cases were reported. Brazil leads the world in the number of dengue cases, with 3.2 million cases and 800 deaths reported in the 2009-14 period.

33. What is the ultimate aim of the project?
A. To release 'good' mosquitoes
B. To reduce the number of people suffering from Dengue Fever
C. To reduce the number of mosquitoes carrying Dengue Fever
D. To reduce the number of people suffering from diseases carried by mosquitoes
E. To follow in Australia's footsteps

34. Which of the following statements would be most damning to the decision to release 'good' mosquitoes?
A. The discovery that Wolbachia has the capacity to mutate such that it can be transmitted to, and will be fatal to, humans
B. The discovery that Wolbachia does not act as a vaccine for Aedes aegypti
C. The discovery that Wolbachia can only be transmitted from male to male mosquitoes
D. The discovery that the evidence from Australia that showed that Wolbachia could not infect humans was tampered with
E. The discovery that Wolbachia can be transmitted to, and causes infertility in, humans

35. Which of the following is not addressed as a potential (but surmountable) issue when releasing mosquitoes?
A. Members of the public panicking about the sudden influx of mosquitoes
B. Wolbachia being transmitted to humans
C. The whole process taking longer than 10 weeks
D. The need for more and more mosquitoes to be released periodically
E. Wolbachia being transmitted to livestock

11. If you're a feminist you'll be called a man-hater. You don't need rebranding

Adapted from 2014© Laurie Penny for the Guardian (edited)

Nobody likes a feminist. At least not according to researchers at the University of Toronto, following a study where it emerged that people still defer to stereotypes about "typical" feminist activists, stereotypes including "man-hating" and "unhygienic". These stereotypes are apparently seriously limiting the appeal of women's liberation as a lifestyle choice. Feminism is a mess, and needs to sort itself out. In order to be "relevant to young women today" it needs to shave its legs and get a haircut.

Elle seems to think so too. The fashion and beauty magazine, not a historically notable manual for gender revolution has weighed in this month with a spread on "rebranding feminism", asking three advertising agencies to give gender politics a nip, tuck and polish. The result is flowcharts and a lot of hot pink equivocation that airbrushes out the ugly, uncomfortable bits of women's liberation. They'd prefer us to consider men's feelings first when we speak about work, pay and sexual violence, to be less threatening, to dress it up; they'd prefer us to talk about "equalism" if we must speak at all. Those with a vested interest in the status quo would prefer young women to act more like they're supposed to – to make everything, including our politics, as pretty and pleasing as possible.

The rebranding of feminism as an aspirational lifestyle choice, a desirable accessory, as easy to adjust to as a detox diet and just as unthreatening, is not a new idea. Nor is ELLE magazine even the first glossy to attempt the task in recent years. But unfortunately there's only so much you can "rebrand" feminism without losing its essential energy, which is difficult, challenging, and full of righteous anger. You can smooth it out and sex it up, but ultimately the reason many people find the word feminism frightening is that it is a fearful thing for anyone invested in male privilege. Feminism asks men to embrace a world where they do not get extra special treats merely because they were born male. Any number of jazzy fonts won't make that easy to swallow.

It is not "young women today" who need to be convinced that feminism remains necessary and "relevant". Changing technology has shaken up a tsunami of activism around gender and politics, from initiatives like the Unslut project and Everyday Sexism to sea changes in culture like the backlash against sexual violence in India. In all of these movements, young women are leading the charge, along with a few fighters from older generations who have not been worn down by decades of mockery and marginalisation. While the fashion press and the beauty industry remain invested in the idea of young women as pliant, affable and terminally anxious about getting boys to like them, real women and girls are fighting back against a culture that persists in trying to present our desires and rebrand our politics as fluffy and marketable.

The stereotype of the ugly, unfuckable feminist exists for a reason – because it's still the last, best line of defence against any woman who is a little too loud, a little too political. Just tell her that if she goes on as she is, nobody will love her. Correct me if I'm wrong, but I've always believed that part of the point of feminist politics – part of the point of any sort of radical politics – is that some principles are more important than being universally adored, particularly by the sort of men who would prefer women to smile quietly and grow our hair out.

In the words of the early suffragist and civil rights campaigner Susan B Anthony: "Cautious, careful people always casting about to preserve their reputation or social standards never can bring about reform. Those who are really in earnest are willing to avow their sympathies with despised ideas and their advocates and bear the consequences."

I am not so very old, but I'm old enough to have noticed that the times in my life when I was most admired by men, the times when I was considered most likeable, were also the times when I was most vulnerable, most powerless and unsure of myself. The times when I've been strongest and most daring, the times when I've been proudest of my own achievements – that's when I've been called a difficult bitch. That's what women get to choose, now as much as at any point in history: how much we are willing to sacrifice to make men like us.

36. All of the following words and phrases suggest disapproval except:
A. 'seriously limiting the appeal of women's liberation'
B. 'has weighed in this week'
C. 'how much we are willing to sacrifice to make men like us'
D. 'the sort of men who would prefer women to smile quietly'
E. 'a lot of hot pink equivocation that airbrushes out the ugly'

37. Why might Laurie Penny uses the word 'jazzy' when describing fonts?
A. To explain to the reader what the fonts look like
B. To draw attention to the illogicality of making feminism more digestible by using the juxtaposition of a seemingly uncomplicated and simple word 'jazzy' against the inherently complex idea of feminism
C. To draw attention to the idea that 'sexing' up the idea of feminism is laughable
D. To belittle what fashion magazines are trying to do
E. All of the above

38. Which of the following phrases can be said to be sarcastic?
A. 'hot pink equivocation that airbrushes out the ugly, uncomfortable bits of women's liberation'
B. '"typical" feminist activitists'
C. 'not a historically notable manual for gender revolution'
D. None of the above
E. All of the above

39. Which of the following is not a description of a feminist found in the extract?
A. Difficult
B. Unsanitary
C. Pliant
D. Relevant
E. Unattractive

12. Complex organic molecule found in interstellar space

Adapted from 2014© Michael Eyre for the BBC (edited)

Scientists have found the beginnings of life-bearing chemistry at the centre of the galaxy.

Iso-propyl cyanide has been detected in a star-forming cloud 27,000 light-years from Earth. Its branched carbon structure is closer to the complex organic molecules of life than any previous finding from interstellar space. The discovery suggests the building blocks of life may be widespread throughout our galaxy.

Various organic molecules have previously been discovered in interstellar space, but i-propyl cyanide is the first with a branched carbon backbone; this is important as it shows that interstellar space could be the origin of more complex branched molecules, such as amino acids, that are necessary for life on Earth.

Dr Arnaud Belloche from the Max Planck Institute for Radio Astronomy is lead author of the research, which appears in the journal Science. "Amino acids on Earth are the building blocks of proteins, and proteins are very important for life as we know it. The question in the background is: is there life somewhere else in the galaxy?"

Watch the skies

The molecule was detected in a giant gas cloud called Sagittarius B2, an active region of ongoing star formation in the centre of the Milky Way. As stars are born in the cloud they heat up microscopic dust grains. Chemical reactions on the surface of the dust allow complex molecules like i-propyl cyanide to form. These molecules emit radiation that was detected as radio waves by twenty 12m telescopes at the Atacama Large Millimeter Array (Alma) in Chile.

Each molecule produces a different "spectral fingerprint" of frequencies. "The game consists in matching these frequencies… to molecules that have been characterised in the laboratory," explained Dr Belloche. "Our goal is to search for new complex organic molecules in the interstellar medium, the ultimate aim is to know whether the elements that are necessary for life to occur… can be found in other places in our galaxy."

Prof. Matt Griffin, head of the school of physics and astronomy at Cardiff University, commented on the discovery. "It's clearly very high-quality data - a very emphatic detection with multiple spectral signatures all seen together.

"There seems to be quite a lot of it, which would indicate that this more complex organic structure is possibly very common, maybe even the norm, when it comes to simple organic molecules in space."

"It's a step closer to discovering molecules that can be regarded as the building blocks or the precursors… of amino acids." The hope is that amino acids will eventually be detected outside our Solar System. "That's what everyone would like to see," said Prof Griffin. If amino acids are widespread throughout the galaxy, life may be also.

"So far we do not have the sensitivity to detect the signals from [amino acids]… in the interstellar medium," explained Dr Belloche. "The interstellar chemistry seems to be able to form these amino acids but at the moment we lack the evidence. […] Alma in the future may be able to do that, once the full capabilities are available."

Prof Griffin agreed this could be the first of many further discoveries from the "fantastically sensitive and powerful" Alma facility.

40. Which of the following best describes Professor Griffin's opinion on the implication of the discovery?
A. It is unremarkable
B. It is a reliable conclusion
C. It is a significant discovery
D. It is unexpected
E. It could be a catalyst for further discovery

41. What is Iso-propyl cyanide?
A. Warmed microscopic dust grains
B. A molecule with a branched carbon backbone
C. Radioactive atoms
D. An organic molecule carrying life
E. A component of an amino acid

42. What can be inferred about amino acids from the extract?
A. In the future, amino acids may be identified outside of the Milky Way
B. The Alma facility could make discoveries at the forefront for molecular science
C. Amino acids are radioactive
D. Amino acids give off signals which are currently undetectable
E. Amino acids are essential for discovering space

END OF SECTION

YOU MUST ANSWER ONLY ONE OF THE FOLLOWING QUESTIONS

Your answer should be a well reasoned argument, showing your understanding of the issue in question and giving the reasons for any opinions you hold.

1. "The government should legalise the sale of human organs" Discuss

2. "Developed countries have a higher obligation to combat climate change than developing countries" Discuss the extent to which you agree with this statement

3. '"Putin is a serious threat to global stability" Discuss

4. "Sufferers of anorexia nervosa should be force fed" Do you agree with this statement? If so, evaluate at what point of an individual's disease this measure should be taken.

END OF TEST

THIS PAGE HAS BEEN

INTENTIONALLY LEFT BLANK

Mock Paper B

1. Water Wars: Egyptians Condemn Ethiopia's Nile Dam Project

Adapted from 2013 © Peter Schwartzstein for National Geographic

As the Grand Ethiopian Renaissance Dam takes shape, tempers rise.

"Ethiopia is killing us," taxi driver Ahmed Hossam said, as he picked his way through Cairo's notoriously traffic-clogged streets. "If they build this dam, there will be no Nile. If there's no Nile, then there's no Egypt."

Projects on the scale of the $4.7 billion, 1.1 mile long (1.7 kilometre long) Grand Ethiopian Renaissance Dam often encounter impassioned resistance, but few inspire the kind of dread and fury with which most Egyptians regard plans to dam the Blue Nile river.
Egypt insists Ethiopia's hydroelectric scheme amounts to a violation of its historic rights, a breach of the 1959 colonial-era agreement that allocated almost three-fourths of the Nile waters to Egypt, and an existential threat to a country largely devoid of alternative freshwater sources.

But what Egyptians regard as a nefarious plot by its historic adversary to control its water supply, Ethiopians see as an intense source of national pride and a symbol of their country's renewal after the debilitating famines of the 1980s and '90s.

"People are enthusiastic. They're excited, because no leader has tried such a project in Ethiopia's history," said Bitania Tadesse, a recent university graduate from the capital, Addis Ababa. "It's a big deal that is going to be beneficial to future generations."

Ethiopia maintains that Egypt and Sudan downstream have no reason to be fearful. The government says it's merely redressing the inequalities of previous water-sharing arrangements, which had left the nine upstream countries largely bereft of access to the Nile.

1. What is implied by the Ethiopian government in the last paragraph?
A. Egypt and Sudan have treated Ethiopia badly in the past
B. Ethiopia has been overlooked in previous water sharing schemes
C. Ethiopia has been purposefully disadvantaged as a result of previous water sharing schemes
D. The Dam is but one retaliation in a long-standing feud between Ethiopia and Egypt
E. Egypt has less need for access to water than Ethiopia does

2. None of the following convey Egypt's distaste for Ethiopia except:
A. 'People are enthusiastic'
B. 'Egypt insists Ethiopia's hydroelectric scheme amounts to a violation of its historic rights'
C. 'Ethiopia is killing us'
D. '(I)mpassioned resistance'
E. 'Egyptians regard as a nefarious plot'

3. Why does Ahmed Hossam use exaggeration in the phrase 'If there is no Nile, there is no Egypt'?
A. He believes that Egypt will cease to exist as a State if the Dam is built
B. He uses stark terms to illustrate how strongly he feels about Ethiopia's decision to build the Dam
C. He hopes to explain how important the Nile is to Egyptian culture
D. He wants to emphasise the severity of the potential problem caused by the Dam
E. He uses sarcasm to belittle the fears of other Egyptians

2. Who is to judge which lives are worth living?

Adapted from 2011 © Barbara Ellen for The Guardian (edited)

The able bodied should never dictate the fates of the ill and weak

There has been some fuss about the forthcoming BBC documentary, *Choosing to Die*, presented by novelist and Alzheimer's sufferer Terry Pratchett, which features a man with motor neurone disease, travelling to Swiss clinic Dignitas and – a first on terrestrial television – dying on screen.

The BBC has been accused of acting "like a cheerleader for legalising assisted suicide", which it denies. Pratchett says: "Everybody possessed of a debilitating and incurable illness should be allowed to pick the hour of their death." Clearly, with him, the dignity of choice is paramount. However, while one has enormous sympathy for Pratchett suffering such a vile disease, the fact remains that he is a rich, powerful man and it is highly unlikely that his wishes would be ignored. With respect, euthanasia laws are not in place to protect people such as him. What of those who may have their "choice" taken away, even if they don't want to die?

There are bigger issues at stake, not least the arrogance of the pro-euthanasia able bodied towards the profoundly ill – the unseemly rush to pronounce the lives of others "not worth living". A recent study discovered that some sufferers of locked-in syndrome – as many as three out of four of the main sample – were happy and did not want to die. Such studies are flawed (some sufferers are unable to articulate either way), but it should still give us pause for thought before blasting off about "lives not worth living".

Likewise the knee-jerk: "They wouldn't have wanted to end up like this." Of course not – who would? – but that might not be the end of the story. How individuals feel when they are fit may change considerably when their health fails. Like those with locked-in syndrome, they may adjust to a life that is very different, often difficult, but just as precious. Who are we to judge?

Bizarrely, the one thing the pro- and anti-euthanasia lobbies have in common is an obsession with God. Sometimes, it's almost as if the antis are tricked into talking about the "sanctity of life" and "God's will", to make the pros look more modern and credible.

Personally, if I ever get something nasty, I'd rather be with a God-botherer than somebody who decides I'm looking peaky, books a Swiss flight and whisks me off to the ghouls at Dignitas. Or maybe I wouldn't – maybe I'd be begging for death. The hope is that I'll choose.

At the moment, assisted death is illegal in Britain, with the caveat that each case is assessed individually, with empathy for the individual and their carers. It could be worse. One reason we don't have the death penalty is that there is no guarantee that mistakes would not be made. Who could guarantee that mistakes wouldn't be made with euthanasia? Not all seriously ill people can communicate their current wishes (not necessarily the same as when they first became ill). And no one else should be deciding for them, in worst-case scenarios "putting them down" against their will.

The phrase: "It's what they would have wanted" belongs after death, not before it. A prolonged, pointlessly agonising end is everyone's nightmare, but that doesn't mean the able bodied should ever get to dictate the fates of the ill and weak. Terry Pratchett should be commended for speaking up for those who wish to die with dignity. However, others who might not want to die, but can't articulate that, need a voice to speak up for them too.

Is this man dead or just dead stupid?

4. What is the main conclusion of the article?
A. The conclusion of Terry Pratchett's documentary is skewed by his own personal circumstances
B. Euthanasia is not yet a precise science and legalising it may give rise to irrevocable mistakes being made
C. Those who have the means to be euthanised should be able to do so if they wish to.
D. Euthanasia should be a personal choice, and legalising euthanasia may give rise to a situation where the seriously ill are robbed of their choice by the healthy
E. Euthanasia could only work if all seriously ill people could articulate their intention to die in such a way that it could not be misunderstood

5. What can be inferred from the discussion of Terry Pratchett's situation?
A. A less wealthy person's wishes are more likely to be ignored
B. Mr Pratchett does not care about those whose choice has been taken away
C. For Mr Fratchett, choice is primarily important
D. A wealthier person's wishes are less likely to be ignored
E. Mr Pratchett is not best placed to discuss any Euthanasia laws

6. Which of the following, if true, would rectify the main problem the author identifies in relation to euthanasia?
A. A law is passed requiring that all people must choose when healthy what they wish to happen to them if they become ill (at varying stages of illness)
B. A new medical procedure is discovered which can analyse the brain's electrical impulses and determine how content a seriously ill patient is
C. Euthanasia is made illegal worldwide, so that even the rich and powerful cannot choose to die
D. A study is published, concluding that 85% of people in a persistent vegetative state will never recover brain function
E. A scientific discovery means that people can be kept alive using life support machine for a fraction of the current cost

7. Why does the author use the phrase 'knee jerk'?
A. To emphasise the importance of evaluating an argument before one makes it
B. To cast doubt upon the value of the argument that follows it
C. To show that, when discussing euthanasia, often people have automatic reactions without truly analysing why they feel this way
D. To suggest that people's reflexive reactions to euthanasia are often wrong
E. To imply that there is no need to make the argument that follows due to it being universally acknowledged to be true

3. Illegal downloaders are one of music industry's biggest customers

Adapted from 2009 © Demos.co.uk

People who use peer-to-peer filesharing websites like Pirate Bay to illegally download music spend over £30 more on music per year than those who do not download illegally.

Internet users who claim to never illegally download music spend an average of £44 per person on music per year, while those who do admit to illegal downloading spend £77, amounting to an estimated £200m in revenue per year.

A new poll commissioned by Demos found that almost one in ten adults (9%) aged 16-50 who have internet access admit downloading music illegally. But this group are also active music buyers, with 8 in 10 buying CDs, vinyl or MP3s in the past year. The poll also found that 42 percent of illegal downloaders agree that they 'like to try things out before I decide whether to buy them.'

The findings suggest that government plans to disconnect repeat illegal downloaders from the internet, announced yesterday by Lord Mandelson, could do the music industry more harm than good by punishing core consumers. The poll showed that the availability of new, appealing legal music provision services is the step most likely to encourage illegal downloaders to stop, above fines or the threat of disconnection.

The research reveals a gap between what consumers are willing to pay for music tracks and current market prices. If official music distribution sites like iTunes lowered the cost of a single track to 45p they could expect prospective buyers to double in number.

Peter Bradwell, a researcher at Demos specialising in digital rights and consumer trends said:

"The latest approach from the government will not help to prop up an ailing music industry. Politicians and music companies need to recognise that the nature of music consumption has changed and consumers are demanding lower prices and easier access to music."

8. Which of the following is true, according to the article?

A. The Government's plans are destined to fail

B. Illegal downloading is not as big a problem as first imagined

C. The poll had surprising results

D. Most people who admit to illegally downloading music also buy music

E. All of the above

9. Which statement (if true) would be most damning to the validity of the poll?

A. Demos' CEO has been charged with tax evasion

B. The participants in the poll were friends of Peter Bradwell

C. Only 25 people were questioned

D. A typo in the questionnaire puts into question how many participants understood exactly what they were being asked

E. Half of the participants were bribed by the government's opposition to lie

10. Which of the following is an assertion of opinion rather than a statement of fact?

A. 'The poll showed that the availability of new, appealing legal music provisions is the step most likely to encourage illegal downloaders to stop

B. 'Politicians and music companies need to recognise that the nature of music consumption has changed'

C. 'The research reveals a gap between what consumers are willing to pay for music trackers and current market prices'

D. '8 in 10 buying CDs, vinyl or MP3s in the last year'

E. 'If official music distribution sites like iTunes lowered the cost of a single track to 45p they could expect prospective buyers to double in number'

4. Heavy Military Recruitment at High Schools Irks Some Parents

Adapted from 2005 © Kelly Beaucar Viahos for FoxNews.com (edited)

A little-known provision in the No Child Left Behind Act that compels public high schools to open their doors and pupil records to military recruiters has some parents, students and anti-war groups up in arms. "We think most people were unaware of it," Amy Hagopian, co-president of the Garfield High School Parent-Teacher-Student Association in Seattle and an active counter-recruiter in the school, said of the provision.

Hagopian said parents are just becoming aware of the policy, which gives recruiters the same access to high school campuses and students' phone numbers and addresses as colleges and businesses have. Districts that don't comply could risk annual federal funding. According to the law, parents must be notified and can refuse to release their children's information. Every school has adopted different notification policies, some being more effective than others, school officials said. Military recruitment issues have been making headlines in recent weeks, as the Army, Marine Corps and National Guard have announced shortfalls in their goals this year. Reports say recruitment pressure is translating into inappropriate tactics by recruiters to the extent that the Army halted recruiting for one day in May to refresh staff with proper protocol in dealing with prospective soldiers.

Paul Rieckoff, an Iraq war veteran and founder of Operation Truth, a veterans' advocacy organization, said parents are now reacting to "major recruiting problems" and bad news coming out of Iraq. "I think it's safe to say there is concern and even the beginning of a movement to combat or to face the recruiters at the high schools," he said. "We don't necessarily endorse that but the critical issue is that the Army has missed their goals again this year." The military has always had access to schools but not all have opened their doors and records equally. Now, the No Child Left Behind Act emboldens efforts to gain "access to the best and brightest this country has to offer," said Department of Defence spokeswoman Lt. Col. Ellen Krenke.

"For some of our students, this may be the best opportunity they have to get a college education," wrote Secretary of Defence Donald Rumsfeld and former Secretary of Education Rod Paige in an October 2002 letter to school superintendents announcing the new law. But some parents and teachers say school is not an appropriate place for the military's message, and complain the hard sell has gotten harder since the Iraq war began and following lacklustre recruitment numbers. "The recruiters really harangue people, and this is what parents are trying to avoid," said Tina Weishaus, president of the Highland Park Middle School/High School Parent Teacher Organization in New Jersey. "Personally, I think the whole thing should be struck from No Child Left Behind," Weishaus said. "I don't think the federal government should be mandating that schools become a recruiting ground for the war."

Army spokesman Doug Smith said the Army has not accelerated recruitment at the schools in the face of missed goals. It is primarily targeting college students, he said, with the average age of 21 for new Army recruits. In 2002, 12,560 out of the 77,000 enlistments were recruited out of high schools. Other critics say they have no problem with military recruiters, but are concerned about students' privacy. According to Montclair school officials, more than 80 percent of the parents who responded to that campaign asked that their records not be given to recruiters this year.

Bill Cala, superintendent of the Fairport Central School District in New York, said his school has been found non-compliant with the law because it doesn't release the names of students to the military unless parents specifically give their consent.

He said about 80 out of the 1,600 students in the school consented this school year, but recruitment among seniors hit 2 percent. "This really, for us, is a privacy issue and doesn't have anything to do with support for the military or for the war," Cala said.

11. Which of the following is a provision of the 'No Child Left Behind' Act?

A. That high schools must give over all the contact information of all their students to military recruiters
B. That high schools are given the option to hand over some students' contact information
C. That high schools must hand over all contact information unless the parents specifically withhold their consent
D. That high schools must give over all students' contact information provided that they have consent from the students to do so
E. That high schools must seek consent from parents before giving over students' contact information to recruiters

12. All of the following are opinions stated in the piece except:

A. The main concern about this provision centres around the students' privacy
B. School is not the right place for military recruitment
C. Recruitment tactics have become inappropriate
D. The recruiters' approach is too aggressive for children in a school environment
E. Most parents are unaware of this specific provision of 'No Child Left Behind'

13. What is the purpose of the inclusion of the phrase 'the hard sell has gotten harder'?

A. The author uses repetition to draw the reader's attention to the idea that recruitment tactics are increasingly rough
B. The author plays on the term 'hard sell' to add variation to the language of the piece
C. The author attempts to be facetious by making fun of the term 'hard sell' to belittle the parents' concerns
D. None of the above
E. All of the above

14. What can be inferred from Bill Cala's figures concerning the number of his students who consented to having their details shared with the military?

A. Most students do not want their details shared with the military
B. Seniors are more likely to consent to having their details shared than younger students
C. Current recruitment strategies are more likely to succeed with older students
D. All of the above
E. Both A and C

5. Found: giant spirals in space that could explain our existence

Adapted from 2015 © Michael Slezak for New Scientist (edited)

Giant magnetic spirals in the sky could explain why there is something rather than nothing in the universe, according to an analysis of data from NASA's Fermi space telescope.
Our best theories of physics imply we shouldn't be here. The Big Bang ought to have produced equal amounts of matter and antimatter particles, which would almost immediately annihilate each other, leaving nothing but light.

So the reality that we are here – and there seems to be very little antimatter around – is one of the biggest unsolved mysteries in physics.

Monopole monopoly

In 2001, Tanmay Vachaspati from Arizona State University offered a purely theoretical solution. Even if matter and antimatter were created in equal amounts, he suggested that as they annihilated each other, they would have briefly created monopoles and antimonopoles – hypothetical particles with just one magnetic pole, north or south.

As the monopoles and antimonopoles in turn annihilated each other, they would produce matter and antimatter. But because of a quirk in nature called CP violation, that process would be biased towards matter, leaving the matter-filled world we see today.
If that happened, Vachaspati showed that there should be a sign of it today: twisted magnetic fields permeating the universe – a fossil of the magnetic monopoles that briefly dominated. And he showed they should look like left-handed screws rather than right-handed screws.

So Vachaspati and his colleagues went looking for them in data from NASA's Fermi Gamma ray Space Telescope. As gamma rays shoot through the cosmos, they should be bent by any magnetic field they pass through, so if there are helical magnetic fields permeating the universe that should leave a visible mark on those gamma rays.

All of a twist

Lo and behold, that's just what they found – well, maybe. "What we found is consistent with them all being left-handed," says Vachaspati. "But we can't be sure." He says there's less than a one per cent chance that what they see in the Fermi data happened by chance. "That's being conservative," he says.

They also found that the twists in the field are a bit bigger than they predicted. "So there is some mystery there," says Vachaspati. He says more data from Fermi, which is expected this year, will help narrow down the odds.

Nicole Bell from the University of Melbourne in Australia warns that magnetic fields could have been caused in other ways, including from inflation. What's more, for CP-violation to provide enough matter in the universe you usually need "new physics" – stuff beyond the standard model of particle physics – which hasn't been confirmed experimentally yet. "But it is a very interesting idea," she says.

15. Which of the following best describes the author's stance in the first paragraph?

A. Human existence is inexplicable

B. Current theories suggest we should not be in existence

C. Our existence can be explained by an analysis of data from NASA's Fermi space telescope

D. The quantities of matter and antimatter particles created during the Big Bang can best explain our existence.

E. Physics will never be able to explain why humans exist

16. The presence of which of the following could indicate helical magnetic fields permeating the universe?

A. Antimatter particles

B. Magnetic monopoles

C. Gamma rays which have been bent by any magnetic field they pass through

D. A mark left on the magnetic field

E. All of the above

17. What does the author mean by "new physics"?

A. Theories beyond the normal model of particle physics

B. Theories which haven't been confirmed by experiments yet

C. Theories which are currently beyond our understanding

D. A and C

E. A and B

6. Making an opinion illegal is not going to stop terrorism

Adapted from 2015 © Jonathan Russell for The Telegraph (edited)

If 'British values' mean anything, they must prevent us from legislating against non-violent views that we find abhorrent

The Government's shift in focus to target extremism and tackle radicalisation rather than counter terrorism is a welcome move, but I question whether the measures set out by the Prime Minister will do this effectively, proportionately and in a way that befits our "British values". Among other things, the proposals are to include "extremism disruption orders", which would not criminalise the act of hate speech or promotion of terrorism, for they are already illegal under the Terrorism Act 2006, but rather the intent to do so, if ministers reasonably believe this to be the case. In essence, these measures target those who operate in what the police have called the "pre-criminal space" and therefore expand the definition of people who could be incarcerated from those who do bad things to those who think bad things. This is problematic for a number of reasons. First, we have the ethical issue of clamping down on freedom of expression, one of our universally accepted human rights. The risk is that the measures are likely to be used in instances when contemplation never graduated to, nor was ever going to graduate to, action. Our courts will have to prosecute entirely on *mens rea* in the absence of *actus reus*, not only an ethically dangerous step towards criminalising thought, but also very difficult in practice to achieve a prosecution in our legal system. The inclusion of "reasonable belief" and a decision by "ministers" likely pre-empts this legal challenge, by having the Home Secretary make judgements rather than the traditional criminal justice system.

Secondly, we risk trying to legislate our way out of the extremist mess our country faces, when we should instead be investing in non-legislative measures to tackle the causes of extremism rather than its symptoms. We have all agreed that "a poisonous ideology" is the root cause and radicalisation is the biggest challenge, yet these measures tackle neither, only serving to disrupt its symptoms – hate preachers on campuses or extremist propaganda disseminators online, for example. A third issue is that we must get beyond simply whacking whichever mole is perceived to be the current nature of the threat. Islamic extremism is like electricity, always seeking to take the path of least resistance. Rather than merely disrupting paths and wasting resources trying to catch up with extremists, we must cut this off at source, and do so without negatively altering the fabric of our nation. The fact that we cannot take water bottles onto planes now is a direct result of the foiled 2006 transatlantic aircraft plot. This will have disrupted future plots and may indeed have made us safer in the last decade, and has done so without clamping down on civil liberties, for carrying water on a plane is not a human right.

But the introduction of Terrorism Investigation and Prevention Measures (TPIMs), which curtail an individual's freedom of movement and freedom of expression without being proven guilty at a fair and public hearing, is problematic because of the failure to uphold the three aforementioned human rights. The measures now being proposed will also fail to strike the correct balance between national security and civil liberties; between counter-terrorism and human rights. Our legislation must be valued and not tinkered with every six months to catch up with the extremist tactics du jour. On top of all of this, it is plain to see that we don't have the capacity within our security services and police force to monitor even more people and enforce an ever-widening set of laws. We increasingly see extremists on the fringes of groups carrying out terrorism-related offences, rather than those at the centre. The new measures might disrupt the communication between those at the centre and those on the fringe, but what we really must do is understand why people are attracted to such groups and their ideologies, and prevent people being vulnerable to radicalisation.

We need a broader, smarter and better financed counter-extremism strategy that engages communities and mobilises civil society to understand and comprehensively challenge the Islamic ideology and refute extremist narratives. The strategy must develop resilience in our institutions and among our young people so we can address their grievances though an alternative secular, democratic, liberal lens. It must also build capacity within our civil society by engaging the private sector and training front line workers, as this is not simply an issue for the state but for all of us. These things combined will truly tackle radicalisation.

18. What is the main conclusion of the article?
A. The Government's proposed measures will be ineffective in tackling radicalisation
B. The Government must pursue a more complex strategy to counter extremism that is flexible enough to change according to the more pressing threat
C. The Government needs to be one step ahead of the terrorists
D. Terrorism can only truly be beaten if the problem is addressed at the source, with measures in place to challenge extremist ideologies in the community
E. The Government's proposed measure would be incompatible with our right to freedom of expression

19. Which of the following is not addressed as a potential problem resulting from the expansion of the law on terrorism?
A. Damaging freedom of expression
B. Extremists moving to the fringes of groups
C. Not confronting a 'poisonous ideology'
D. Difficulties in implementation (lack of resources)
E. Paternalism being taken too far

20. Why does the author use the example of Islamic extremism being 'like electricity'?
A. To scare the reader by emphasising the depth of extremist infiltration of society
B. To explain how information is shared amongst extremist groups
C. To emphasise how flexible extremists can be at finding new methods to spread their message
D. To support his point that the government will fail if they continue to address each new issues as it arises
E. To explain why the new measures will not work

21. Which of the following is a statement of fact, rather than an assertion of opinion?
A. 'the proposals are to include "extremism disruption orders", which would not criminalise the act of hate speech'
B. 'it is plain to see that we don't have the capacity'
C. 'We need a broader, smarter and better financed counter extremism strategy'
D. 'the inclusion of "reasonable belief" and a decision by "ministers" likely pre-empts this legal challenge'
E. 'we should instead be investing in non-legislative measures to tackle the causes of extremism rather than its symptoms'

7. Does Death Penalty Save Lives? A New Debate

Adapted from 2007 © Adam Liptak for The New York Times (edited)

For the first time in a generation, the question of whether the death penalty deters murders has captured the attention of scholars in law and economics, setting off an intense new debate about one of the central justifications for capital punishment. According to roughly a dozen recent studies, executions save lives. For each inmate put to death, the studies say, 3 to 18 murders are prevented. "I personally am opposed to the death penalty," said H. Naci Mocan, an author of a study finding that each execution saves five lives. "But my research shows that there is a deterrent effect." The studies have been the subject of sharp criticism, much of it from legal scholars who say that the theories of economists do not apply to the violent world of crime and punishment. Critics of the studies say they are based on faulty premises, insufficient data and flawed methodologies.

The death penalty "is applied so rarely that the number of homicides it can plausibly have caused or deterred cannot reliably be disentangled from the large year-to-year changes in the homicide rate caused by other factors," John J. Donohue III, a law professor at Yale with a doctorate in economics. But the studies have started to reshape the debate over capital punishment and to influence prominent legal scholars. "The evidence on whether it has a significant deterrent effect seems sufficiently plausible that the moral issue becomes a difficult one," said Cass R. Sunstein, a law professor at the University of Chicago who has frequently taken liberal positions. "I did shift from being against the death penalty to thinking that if it has a significant deterrent effect it's probably justified."

Professor Sunstein and Adrian Vermeule, a law professor at Harvard, wrote in their own Stanford Law Review article that "Capital punishment may well save lives. Those who object to capital punishment, and who do so in the name of protecting life, must come to terms with the possibility that the failure to inflict capital punishment will fail to protect life." There is also a classic economics question lurking in the background, Professor Wolfers said. "Capital punishment is very expensive," he said, "so if you choose to spend money on capital punishment you are choosing not to spend it somewhere else, like policing." A single capital litigation can cost more than $1 million. It is at least possible that devoting that money to crime prevention would prevent more murders than whatever number, if any, an execution would deter.

The available data is admittedly thin, mostly because there are so few executions. In 2003, for instance, there were more than 16,000 homicides but only 153 death sentences and 65 executions. "It seems unlikely," Professor Donohue and Professor Wolfers concluded in their Stanford article, "that any study based only on recent U.S. data can find a reliable link between homicide and execution rates." The two professors offered one particularly compelling comparison. Canada has executed no one since 1962. Yet the murder rates in the United States and Canada have moved in close parallel since then, including before, during and after the four-year death penalty moratorium in the United States in the 1970s.

"Deterrence cannot be achieved with a half-hearted execution program," Professor Shepherd of Emory wrote in the Michigan Law Review in 2005. She found a deterrent effect in only those states that executed at least nine people between 1977 and 1996.

Professor Wolfers said the answer to the question of whether the death penalty deterred was "not unknowable in the abstract," given enough data. "If I was allowed 1,000 executions and 1,000 exonerations, and I was allowed to do it in a random, focused way," he said, "I could probably give you an answer."

22. Which of the following, if true, would be most compelling in support of the idea that the death penalty does save lives?

A. A study concludes that 80% of murderers do not understand the personal implications of their actions
B. A larger study was undertaken showing a higher degree of correlation between dropping murder rates and death sentences
C. A study determines that 70% of murders are premeditated
D. The comparison between Canada and the United States is proven to have been falsified
E. A survey was circulated to hundreds of thousands of free citizens. 59% of them suggested that they would be less likely to kill someone if they knew that there was a possibility they might be executed as a result

23. What can be inferred from Professor Sunstein and Adrian Wolfers' discussion in the Stanford article?

A. Choosing not to inflict capital punishment may not result in lives being saved
B. It is unlikely that those who oppose the death penalty will change their minds following this research
C. Those who support capital punishment will be troubled by this research
D. The authors believe that those who oppose capital punishment may do so without much thought as to why
E. Murderers on death row will want this information to be circulated

24. Why does the author use the word 'admittedly' in the statement 'The available data is *admittedly* thin, mostly because there are so few executions'

A. He wants to show that the studies are worthy of discussion, despite not having many participants
B. He wants to emphasise what his personal opinion is, whilst taking notice of the opposition
C. He knows he must share the opposition to his own argument, but wants to do so whilst maintaining his own opinion
D. He wants to show reluctance in sharing the opposition argument as he knows it has merit and could weaken his point
E. All of the above

25. What, on balance, does the article suggest is the main reason these studies have attracted criticism?

A. Economic theories do not apply in real-life situations
B. The method under which these conclusions were drawn was flawed
C. The studies consider capital punishment in abstraction and do not compare with other options such as crime prevention
D. The authors who have undertaken them have been the subject of professional criticism
E. There is not enough available data to conclude whether or not capital punishment has a deterrent effect

8. The answer to Britain's economic woes? Make pensioners work longer

Adapted from 2015 © Lauren Davidson and Peter Spence for The Telegraph (edited)

The UK could have a stronger economy if it encouraged its older population to stay in the workforce, a new report has found.

The World Economic Forum has ranked the UK 19th out of 124 nations on an index that measures how well countries "nurture, develop and deploy their great asset – its people" with a focus on education, skills and employment. With an overall score of 79.07%, the UK capitalises on its population better than such economic powerhouses as Germany and China, but fails to match up to many of its peers including the US, France and Japan.

The UK slipped down the index because of its weak score in the 65 and over age group, coming 47th in this category, dragged down by a particularly low labour force participation rate of 10.2% that saw 86 other countries fare better than the UK.

An unemployment rate of 3.7%, ranking the UK just 38th on the global index, suggests that the silver population is lacking in job opportunities for those who want to work.

"There's always a lot of focus on youth unemployment and disillusionment which has a long term effect on a country," Saadia Zahidi, head of the WEF's Employment, Skills and Human Capital Initiative and co-author of the report, said. "But the same issue applies to women and older workers as well."

The average age of retirement in the UK is 64.7 for men and 63.1 for women, but ministers believe it should be higher to prevent healthcare and pensions crises caused by the ageing population and have previously indicated that they would like the average retirement age to rise by as much as six months every year. A recent report from the Department for Work and Pensions found that an extra £25bn would be generated if just half of the older people seeking work were given jobs.

"Talent, not capital, will be the key factor linking innovation, competitiveness and growth in the 21st century," said Klaus Schwab, founder and executive chairman of the World Economic Forum. "To make any of the changes necessary to unlock the world's latent talent – and hence its growth potential – we must look beyond campaign cycles and quarterly reports."

Finland topped the ranking, which the WEF claims is the only global report of its kind, with a score of 85.78%, followed by Norway and Switzerland. Canada, which is the world's best at maximising its 15 to 24 age group, took fourth place, while Japan rounded out the top five thanks to its chart-topping deployment of people over the age of 65.

Julio A. Portalatin, president and chief executive officer of Mercer, which produced the report in collaboration with the WEF, called the Index "a critical tool for global employers".
He said: "It allows them to determine the most pressing issues impacting talent availability and suitability around the world today and identify those issues that have the potential to impact business success in the future – invaluable insight for guiding the allocation of workforce development and investments."

26. Which of the following is an assumption that the authors have made?
A. The UK focuses too much attention on youth unemployment
B. Most over 65's currently out of work would like to work if the opportunity arose for them to do so
C. The figures suggest that there are not enough job opportunities available for over 65's (as opposed to over 65's just not wanting to work)
D. Finland, Norway and Switzerland properly utilise their ageing population
E. Talent is more important than capital to ensure a stable economy

27. Which of the following most accurately describes the index identified in the extract?
A. A critical tool for global employers
B. An indication of how efficiently countries utilise their population within the economy
C. A method by which a country's education, skills and employment are evaluated
D. A source of insight to help allocation of investment in countries' workforces
E. A set of figures which shows how successful countries are at providing opportunities for their ageing workforce

28. What does Klaus Schwab imply in his discussion of the value of talent?
A. Campaign cycles and quarterly reports are an inefficient use of time
B. Talent is more important than capital
C. Those who look only to campaign systoles and quarterly reports are naive
D. The world will not be able to meet its potential for growth unless unutilised talent is eliminated
E. Quarterly reports are useless

9. Deadly Frog Fungus Pops Up in Madagascar, An Amphibian Wonderland

Adapted from 2015 © Jane Lee for National Geographic

Madagascar has been spared the scourge of the chytrid fungus, until recently.

Madagascar is home to a mind-boggling array of frogs, 99 percent of which are found nowhere else in the world. But a study released Thursday finds the island nation now also hosts the greatest threat to amphibian biodiversity in modern times—the chytrid fungus.

As many as 7 percent of the world's amphibian species live only in Madagascar, says Molly Bletz, a researcher at the Braunschweig University of Technology in Germany. Chytrid is responsible for the decline or extinction of hundreds of amphibian species around the world. One forest in Panama lost 30 amphibian species to the fungus in about a year, according to a 2010 study.

Why It Matters

Researchers had thought Madagascar was chytrid-free. A 2014 study found chytrid on Madagascar frogs shipped to the U.S. for the pet trade, but researchers weren't sure whether the animals were contaminated en route or infected in Madagascar.

But a new study in the journal *Scientific Reports* finds that chytrid is present in multiple Madagascar frog species. Bletz and colleagues examined skin swabs and tissue samples from 4,155 amphibians tested for chytrid from 2005 to 2014. They found, to their surprise, that the fungus began to appear on frogs starting in 2010. What they haven't found yet is sick frogs. "It could mean we just caught it very early," Bletz says, or it's possible the chytrid strain in Madagascar isn't very lethal.

The Big Picture

"It's the best worst-case scenario," says Jonathan Kolby, a researcher at Queensland's James Cook University, who was not involved in the study. "[Chytrid] is there, but the frogs aren't dying right now."

Scientists need to figure out where the chytrid came from, though, he says. If it was introduced, scientists need to know how it got into the country and how they can prevent another introduction. "Because next time, it could be a strain that's supervirulent," says Kolby, a National Geographic grantee.

What's Next

Meanwhile, experts are working on a multipronged response to the threat. Bletz is working on a possible preventive treatment using frog skin bacteria that may fight off the fungal invader. Other groups around the world—such as in Panama—are setting up breeding facilities for especially vulnerable amphibians just in case, while others in places including Madagascar and Panama are working on long-term amphibian monitoring efforts.

29. Which of the following best describes Jonathan Kolby's approach to the situation in Madagascar?
A. Optimistic
B. Cautiously Relieved
C. Pessimistic
D. Concerned
E. Prudent

30. What can be inferred about chytrid from the article?
A. It takes some time to kill frogs
B. It is supervirulent
C. It is a fungus
D. It is harmful to all amphibians
E. It is not harmful to frogs

31. Which of the following are mentioned in the article as being worked on as a response to the threat?
A. A prophylactic treatment
B. Developing reproduction centres for vulnerable Madagascan frogs
C. Improving observation procedures
D. B and C
E. A and C

10. Why presume a child raised by a gay couple will be emotionally damaged?

Adapted from 2015 © Eleanor Morgan for The Guardian (edited)

In the summer holidays before my 14th birthday, my mum told my siblings and I that my dad would be leaving because she'd begun a relationship with her friend – a woman. I remember the scene clearly; Mum sat on the bottom bunk and told us, calmly, what had happened and what was going to happen now. We cried. We shouted. I ran out of the room screaming at her while my sister gingerly cuddled her.

It's gut-wrenching, whatever the circumstances, to watch your dad pack his things into sports bags and leave the family home. In a fit of utterly emo teenageness I made myself listen to John Lennon's Jealous Guy again and again on my Discman until I could cry out my frustration. I laugh now when I remember writing "I was shivering inside" at the back of my school organiser. But I was. My teenage heart hurt, too, when we'd spend weekends at his temporary bedsit in Chigwell and wake up in the night on our blow-up lilo to see him looking at us with watery eyes. But aren't these experiences par for the course of any parental separation? I had fears and prejudices relating to my mum's new relationship: what will I tell my friends? (I didn't, for ages.) What will the neighbours think? What will people think if we go on holiday together? But looking back, despite my desperate sadness, the gender shift in the house was never really a black cloud. It was the idea of someone else full stop.

This is partly why I have found pieces like Hetty Baynes' in the Daily Mail, detailing how being raised by two mums "ruined her life", and this open letter-style piece that says "Dear gay community: your kids are hurting" so uncomfortable. The layers of irresponsibility in the Daily Mail article are myriad, and while Baynes may well be damaged by her upbringing and feel justified speaking about her family in such a way, the poison dart for me is the line, "So how to explain the bizarre construct which passed for my family?"

When adults are emotionally neglectful of children – as Baynes says her mother and her female lover were of her – it can be harmful and you can end up firing your blame in all sorts of directions. But is being emotionally neglectful a gender-specific thing? I don't think so. If a woman isn't considering the needs of her daughter properly, it's not because she's gay or bisexual – these things are multi-causal and cannot, must not, be hung on the idea of gayness somehow poisoning the ability for normal love and rationality.

I had some really horrible times in the house we shared with my mum's partner, her two children and my brother and sister. Two women, five children. There were, as Baynes experienced, lots of people vying for space and prominence. There was resentment, jealousy and incidents that did cause long-term damage, but they happened as a result of two families being thrown into a building together. When I finally told my friends at school (the excuses for not having them round were wearing thin) the ones whose parents had separated and who had new family dynamics all spoke of similar problems. My problems were not unique because my step-parent figure was a woman.

I experience a crisis whenever I read any of these pieces because for every encouraging study that says the children of gay parents are doing all right we have these singular accounts of pain and turmoil attributed to homosexuality. Everyone is entitled to portray their pain how they wish, but at what point do we say, as a society, that using a public platform to make gross generalisations like Baynes does when she says "roll the dice … you are taking a chance with an innocent life" is harmful?

Although perhaps not to the same degree, I feel the same way today as I did when Dolce and Gabbana made their hateful, dehumanising remarks about "synthetic" IVF children in an interview, because such insular considerations, in such a visible context, are shameful. Talking about your own experience definitely falls under the free speech banner, but making blanket remarks about what is and isn't safe for a child doesn't.

As someone who was co-parented by two women for a while, and who is in a same-sex relationship and planning to have IVF to conceive a child some day, seeing these things splashed across front pages makes my insides curdle. I can laugh at the absurdity, but still know that, however much progress we've made, so many people will agree. That's what's frightening.

32. All of the following suggest disapproval except:
A. 'gross generalisations'
B. 'dehumanising remarks'
C. 'layers of irresponsibility'
D. 'gut-wrenching'
E. 'insular considerations'

33. Which of the following is true according to the author?
A. Her teenage reaction to her parents' news was unjustified
B. None of the problems the author encountered were due to having same sex guardians
C. The problems she encountered as a teenager was due to two families being pushed together in a new and difficult scenario
D. People should be able to speak freely about inferences about the wider world they can draw from their own personal experiences
E. Neglectfulness in a same-sex household is more often than not due to resentment

34. What assumption does the author make in the piece?
A. There is no scenario in which a child might be happy to see a father leave the family home
B. Resentment is a logical response to family upheaval
C. Dolce and Gabbana must feel similarly negatively towards same-sex unions
D. Had her father been around, she would have been happier
E. IVF children are less 'human' than other children

35. Why might Eleanor Morgan use the term 'poison dart' in relation to Baynes' argument?
A. To explain the importance of this particular part of Baynes' argument
B. To draw attention to the fact that Baynes' argument is flawed
C. To draw attention to the fact that Baynes is unjustified in extending her argument so far
D. To draw attention to the fact that the author finds Baynes' article distasteful
E. All of the above

11. Calculated risks: Will algorithms make business boring?

Adapted from 2015 © Zoe Kleinman for BBC News (edited)

Ever found yourself wondering whether your boss is human?

Haven't we all.

Now, with the march of artificial intelligence and robotics, it's becoming an increasingly valid question. Algorithms – problem solving computer programmes – are, to put it bluntly, getting much better at doing our jobs than we are. And it's not just in the tech sector where computers are becoming king, school children in South Korea are being taught English by a machine called Robosem.

But is there a danger that this brave new world is going to be a bit, well, dull?

Movies by numbers

The entertainment industry has already adopted an algorithmic approach to working out what we want to watch. When TV and movie streaming service Netflix decided to start commissioning its own material, it turned not to Hollywood veterans, film critics or media forecasters, but to algorithms and user data.

A data trawl of the most-watched and loved content streamed by Netflix customers revealed three key ingredients - actor Kevin Spacey, director David Fincher and political dramas produced by the BBC. So the firm commissioned a remake of 1990 BBC political thriller House of Cards, starring Kevin Spacey and directed by David Fincher. It became the first ever web series to win a prestigious Emmy award, with the first series receiving nine nominations.

High tech traders

The finance sector is another enjoying the comparative stability of computer control.

"The trading floor was a very exciting place. Now it's more like a software company than a financial organisation," said Dr Juan Pablo Pardo-Guerra, assistant professor at the London School of Economics.

High-frequency financial trader Virtu, an electronic trader with computerised strategies, has only ever recorded one day of losses in nearly six years. On its website the firm claims that its 148 employees are the "secret sauce" of its success but its own proprietary technology is at the heart of all of its trading activity.

Financial thrill-seekers will still enjoy working in the sector, predicts Dr Pardo-Guerra – but there will definitely be a change of scene. "It's probably going to have some impact on how people relate with the market, how they find excitement in trading," he said.

And the good news is there is still room for the human touch – at least for now.

"Even within the most analytical part of finance, meetings and relationships are still quite important and that's something algorithms can't do," he added. "Some aspects can be automated – calculated or quantitative decision making. But others rely more on personal cues and networks."

Algorithms have another potentially fatal flaw – they are unable to recognise when someone is taking the tricks of the trade too far.

"People know how to manipulate prices to get more customers or make their strategies more profitable," said Dr Pardo-Guerra. "I think algorithms present challenges in terms of identifying these processes."

36. Why might the author choose to start the piece in this way?
A. To grab the audience's attention
B. To establish an informal register from the beginning
C. To immediately create a connection with the audience
D. All of the above
E. A and C

37. Which of the following is not identified in the piece as an example of artificial intelligence being used to make our lives easier?
A. Computers being used to teach children
B. Algorithms being used to predict human behaviour
C. Automating quantitative decision making
D. Strategising trading decisions
E. Algorithms being used to develop products

38. What is the main reason is it suggested that artificially intelligent beings are inferior to human beings in certain roles?
A. They cannot build relationships and trust with other humans
B. They are unable to identify and respond to uniquely human reactions
C. They take tricks of the trade too far
D. They cannot identify when a human is playing outside of the rules
E. Their efficacy will result in business becoming dull

39. What does the author imply in the piece about the future of business?
A. It will be computer-centric
B. It will be more efficient
C. It might become tedious
D. Humans will still be necessary for certain tasks
E. All of the above

12. U.S. opposes honest labelling of GMO foods

Adapted from 2010 © Ethan Huff for Natural News

The official U.S. position on genetically-modified organisms, also known as GMs or GMOs, is that there is no difference between them and natural organisms. Crafted by the U.S. Food and Drug Administration (FDA) and the Department of Agriculture (USDA), the position set forth to the Codex Alimentarius Commission on the issue goes even further to suggest that no country should be able to require mandatory GMO labelling on food items, even though science shows that GMOs act differently in the body than do natural organisms and are a threat to health.

A group of over 80 food processors, farmers and consumer organizations has sent an official letter to Michael Taylor, deputy commission at the FDA, and Kathleen Merrigan, deputy secretary of agriculture at the USDA, protesting the official U.S. position, citing the fact that it creates "significant problems" for all U.S. food producers that wish to label their products as being GMO-free.

Not only is there no mandatory labelling of products sold in the U.S. that contain GMO ingredients, but the FDA and USDA now want to prohibit the labelling of products that do not contain GMO ingredients. In other words, the FDA and USDA are trying to outlaw truth in labelling and are openly working deceive the public.

Among those opposing the draft U.S. position on GMOs are members of the Consumers Union, the Organic Trade Association, the Union of Concerned Scientists and the Centre for Food Safety.

The FDA and USDA actually had the audacity to include in the draft position that mandatory labelling of GMOs is "false, misleading [and] deceptive" because it implies that there is a difference between GMO ingredients and non-GMO ingredients.

Fortunately, science and pure common sense, which are both lacking at the FDA and USDA, indicate that GMOs are different from non-GMOs, and that the public has a right to know the types of ingredients that are in the products they buy.

Many countries already require food processors and manufacturers to label products that contain GMOs, but the FDA and USDA hope to convince the Codex Committee to outlaw this practice.

Not only are GMOs structurally different than non-GMOs, but GMOs are actually toxic. Several studies have shown that they are harmful to the body.

40. What, according to the article, is the U.S. position on GMOs?
A. They are identical to natural organisms
B. No country should be able to demand labelling on products identifying them as GMOs
C. There is no distinction between them and natural organisms
D. A and B
E. B and C

41. Which of the following would best describe the author's perception of the U.S. position?
A. Evasive
B. Obstructive
C. Impudent
D. Illogical
E. Competent

42. Which of the following, if true, would most undermine the author's position?
A. The 'several studies' he mentions in the final paragraph are proven to have been falsified
B. The U.S position is supported by 90% of MEDC countries around the globe
C. The U.S has used no scientific evidence to support its position
D. The author is proven to be a fanatical eco-terrorist
E. An article published in the New Scientist magazine supports the idea that GMOs act no differently to biological organisms

END OF SECTION

YOU MUST ANSWER <u>ONLY</u> <u>ONE</u> OF THE FOLLOWING QUESTIONS

Your answer should be a well reasoned argument, showing your understanding of the issue in question and giving the reasons for any opinions you hold.

1. Tennessee currently protects teachers who wish to teach children to explore the potential value of following creationism. Do you think that this is correct? Identify and analyse any legal problems that may arise in discussion of this law.

2. "There is a time and a place for censorship of the internet." Discuss with particular reference to the right of freedom of expression.

3. "The UK should codify its Constitution' Discuss.

4. "The general trend towards the liberalisation of marriage undermines its religious basis." Discuss this comment with reference to the idea of abolishing marriage as a legal concept.

END OF TEST

THIS PAGE HAS BEEN

INTENTIONALLY LEFT BLANK

Mock Paper C

1. Marriage

Ever since the time, nineteen years ago, when Mrs Mona Caird attacked the institution of matrimony in the Westminster Review and led the way for the great discussion on 'Is Marriage a Failure?' in the Daily Telegraph—marriage has been the hardy perennial of newspaper correspondence, and an unfailing resource to worried sub-editors. When seasons are slack and silly, the humblest member of the staff has but to turn out a column on this subject, and whether it be a serious dissertation on 'The Perfections of Polygamy' or a banal discussion on 'Should Husbands have Tea at Home?', it will inevitably achieve the desired result, and fill the spare columns of the papers with letters for weeks to come. People are always interested in matrimony, whether from the objective or subjective point of view, and that is my excuse for perpetrating yet another book on this well-worn, but ever fertile topic.

Marriage indeed seems to be in the air more than ever in this year of grace; everywhere it is discussed, and very few people seem to have a good word to say for it. The most superficial observer must have noticed that there is being gradually built up in the community a growing dread of the conjugal bond, especially among men; and a condition of discontent and unrest amongst married people, particularly women. What is the matter with this generation that wedlock has come to assume so distasteful an aspect in their eyes? On every side one hears it vilified and its very necessity called into question. From the pulpit, the clergy endeavour to uphold the sanctity of the institution, and unceasingly exhort their congregations to respect it and abide by its laws. But the Divorce Court returns make ominous reading; every family solicitor will tell you his personal experience goes to prove that happy unions are considerably on the decrease, and some of the greatest thinkers of our day join in a chorus of condemnation against latter-day marriage.

Tolstoy says: 'the relations between the sexes are searching for a new form, the old one is falling to pieces.' Among the manuscript 'remains' of Ibsen, the profound student of human nature, the following noteworthy passage occurs: '"free-born men" is a phrase of rhetoric. They do not exist, for marriage, the relation between man and wife, has corrupted the race and impressed the mark of slavery upon all. 'Not long ago, too, our greatest living novelist, George Meredith, created an immense sensation by his suggestion that marriage should become a temporary arrangement, with a minimum lease of, say, ten years.

That the time has not yet come for any such revolutionary change is obvious, but if the signs and portents of the last decade or two do not lie, we may safely assume that the time will come, and that the present legal conditions of wedlock will be altered in some way or other.

1. The writer takes the view that:
A. Marriage needs to undergo a revolutionary change now
B. Marriage will not require a change at all
C. Marriage will undergo a change in the future
D. Marriage will become a temporary arrangement
E. Marriage is in decline

2. What does Tolstoy suggest?
A. Marriage as a concept is outdated
B. People do not believe in marriage anymore
C. Marriage is on a steady decline
D. The concept of adult relationships is evolving
E. Couples no longer wish to get married

3. What does the writer **not** suggest in the first paragraph?
A. Marriage is an important topic for people
B. Marriage is an interesting topic for people
C. Marriage provides good fodder for publications
D. There are both serious and trivial publications on marriage
E. Marriage has been discussed very frequently in publications

4. Which word is **not** used by the writer as a form of criticism?
A. Hardy
B. Silly
C. Banal
D. Superficial
E. Distasteful

2. Nature or nurture?

Galton adopted and popularised Shakespeare's antithesis of nature and nurture to describe a man's inheritance and his surroundings, the two terms including everything that can pertain to a human being. The words are not wholly suitable, particularly since nature has two distinct meanings, — human nature and external nature. The first is the only one considered by Galton. Further, nurture is capable of subdivision into those environmental influences which do not undergo much change, — e.g., soil and climate, — and those forces of civilization and education which might better be described as culture. The evolutionist has really to deal with the three factors of germ-plasm, physical surroundings and culture. But Galton's phrase is so widely current that we shall continue to use it, with the implications that have just been outlined.

The antithesis of nature and nurture is not a new one; it was met long ago by biologists and settled by them to their own satisfaction. The whole body of experimental and observational evidence in biology tends to show that the characters which the individual inherits from his ancestors remain remarkably constant in all ordinary conditions to which they may be subjected. Their constancy is roughly proportionate to the place of the animal in the scale of evolution; lower forms are more easily changed by outside influence, but as one ascends to the higher forms, which are more differentiated, it is found more and more difficult to effect any change in them. Their characters are more definitely fixed at birth.

It is with the highest of all forms, Man, that we have now to deal. The student in biology is not likely to doubt that the differences in men are due much more to inherited nature than to any influences brought to bear after birth, even though these latter influences include such powerful ones as nutrition and education within ordinary limits.

But the biological evidence does not lend itself readily to summary treatment, and we shall therefore examine the question by statistical methods. These have the further advantage of being more easily understood; for facts which can be measured and expressed in numbers are facts whose import the reader can usually decide for himself: he is perfectly able to determine, without any special training, whether twice two does or does not make four. One further preliminary remark: the problem of nature vs. nurture cannot be solved in general terms; a moment's thought will show that it can be understood only by examining one trait at a time. The problem is to decide whether the differences between the people met in everyday life are due more to inheritance or to outside influences, and these differences must naturally be examined separately; they cannot be lumped together.

5. The writer suggests in the first paragraph that:
A. We should no longer use the terms 'nature or nurture'
B. Galton created the terms 'nature or nurture'
C. Galton uses the terms 'nature or nurture' precisely
D. 'Nurture' does not undergo much change
E. 'Nature or nurture' is very widely used

6. Why does the writer capitalise the word 'man' in the third paragraph?
A. It is the official name of a species
B. The writer wants to emphasise its importance
C. The writer is not using the word's ordinary meaning
D. The writer wants to refer to a collective group
E. The writer is referring to a particular person

7. The writer is of the view that:
A. We should analyse 'nature or nurture' as a whole
B. We should only focus on one trait at a time
C. Nature plays a bigger part than nurture as shown by biology
D. It is difficult to change what is inherited by man
E. Statistical methods will provide a more accurate answer than summary methods

8. Which of the following pair of words are **not** used as a contrasting pair?
A. Inheritance and surroundings
B. Human nature and external nature
C. Soil and climate
D. Lower forms and higher forms
E. Inheritance and outside influences

3. Biology

I must at the outset remark that among the many sciences that are occupied with the study of the living world there is no one that may properly lay exclusive claim to the name of Biology. The word does not, in fact, denote any particular science but is a generic term applied to a large group of biological sciences all of which alike are concerned with the phenomena of life. To present in a single address, even in rudimentary outline, the specific results of these sciences is obviously an impossible task, and one that I have no intention of attempting. I shall offer no more than a kind of preface or introduction to those who will speak after me on the biological sciences of physiology, botany and zoology; and I shall confine it to what seem to me the most essential and characteristic of the general problems towards which all lines of biological inquiry must sooner or later converge.

It is the general aim of the biological sciences to learn something of the order of nature in the living world. Perhaps it is not amiss to remark that the biologist may not hope to solve the ultimate problems of life any more than the chemist and physicist may hope to penetrate the final mysteries of existence in the non-living world. What he can do is to observe, compare and experiment with phenomena, to resolve more complex phenomena into simpler components, and to this extent, as he says, to "explain" them; but he knows in advance that his explanations will never be in the full sense of the word final or complete. Investigation can do no more than push forward the limits of knowledge.

The task of the biologist is a double one. His more immediate effort is to inquire into the nature of the existing organism, to ascertain in what measure the complex phenomena of life as they now appear are capable of resolution into simpler factors or components, and to determine as far as he can what is the relation of these factors to other natural phenomena. It is often practically convenient to consider the organism as presenting two different aspects—a structural or morphological one, and a functional or physiological—and biologists often call themselves accordingly morphologists or physiologists. Morphological investigation has in the past largely followed the method of observation and comparison, physiological investigation that of experiment; but it is one of the best signs of progress that in recent years the fact has come clearly into view that morphology and physiology are really inseparable, and in consequence the distinctions between them, in respect both to subject matter and to method, have largely disappeared in a greater community of aim.

If I have the temerity to draw your attention to the fundamental problem towards which all lines of biological inquiry sooner or later lead us, it is not with the delusion that I can contribute anything new to the prolonged discussions and controversies to which it has given rise. I desire only to indicate in what way it affects the practical efforts of biologists to gain a better understanding of the living organism, whether regarded as a group of existing phenomena or as a product of the evolutionary process; and I shall speak of it, not in any abstract or speculative way, but from the standpoint of the working naturalist. The problem of which I speak is that of organic mechanism and its relation to that of organic adaptation. How in general are the phenomena of life related to those of the non-living world? How far can we profitably employ the hypothesis that the living body is essentially an automaton or machine, a configuration of material particles, which, like an engine or a piece of clockwork, owes its mode of operation to its physical and chemical construction? It is not open to doubt that the living body is a machine. It is a complex chemical engine that applies the energy of the food-stuffs to the performance of the work of life. But is it something more than a machine? If we may imagine the physico-chemical analysis of the body to be carried through to the very end, may we expect to find at last an unknown something that transcends such analysis and is neither a form of physical energy nor anything given in the physical or chemical configuration of the body? Shall we find anything corresponding to the usual popular conception—which was also along the view of physiologists—that the body is "animated" by a specific "vital principle," or "vital force," a dominating "archæus" that exists only in the realm of organic nature? If such a principle exists, then the mechanistic hypothesis fails and the fundamental problem of biology becomes a problem sui generis.

9. The writer is of the view that:
A. Biology is more worthy of study than physics or chemistry
B. Biology only consists of physiology, botany and zoology
C. The sciences can be split into the living and non-living
D. Biology is the only study of the living world
E. Biology consists of many different sciences concerned with life

10. Which of the following, according to the passage, is a **fact**?
A. Biology lays exclusive claim to the study of the living world
B. To present in a single address, even in rudimentary outline, the specific results of these sciences is obviously an impossible task
C. It is the general aim of the biological sciences to learn something of the order of nature in the living world
D. The biologist may not hope to solve the ultimate problems of life any more than the chemist and physicist may hope to penetrate the final mysteries of existence in the non-living world
E. It is often practically convenient to consider the organism as presenting two different aspects—a structural or morphological one, and a functional or physiological

11. Which of the following does the writer believe biologists are **not** able to offer a solution?
A. 'The phenomena of life'
B. 'Order of nature in the living world'
C. 'The ultimate problems of life'
D. 'Nature of the existing organism'
E. 'resolve more complex phenomena into simpler components'

12. Which of the following rhetorical questions do **not** refer or relate to a metaphorical analysis?
A. How in general are the phenomena of life related to those of the non-living world?
B. How far can we profitably employ the hypothesis that the living body is essentially an automaton or machine, a configuration of material particles, which, like an engine or a piece of clockwork, owes its mode of operation to its physical and chemical construction?
C. But is it something more than a machine?
D. If we may imagine the physico-chemical analysis of the body to be carried through to the very end, may we expect to find at last an unknown something that transcends such analysis and is neither a form of physical energy nor anything given in the physical or chemical configuration of the body?
E. Shall we find anything corresponding to the usual popular conception—which was also along the view of physiologists—that the body is "animated" by a specific "vital principle," or "vital force," a dominating "archæus" that exists only in the realm of organic nature?

4. Fossils

Fossils are the remains, or even the indications, of animals and plants that have, through natural agencies, been buried in the earth and preserved for long periods of time. This may seem a rather meagre definition, but it is a difficult matter to frame one that will be at once brief, exact, and comprehensive; fossils are not necessarily the remains of extinct animals or plants, neither are they, of necessity, objects that have become petrified or turned into stone.

Bones of the Great Auk and Rytina, which are quite extinct, would hardly be considered as fossils; while the bones of many species of animals, still living, would properly come in that category, having long ago been buried by natural causes and often been changed into stone. And yet it is not essential for a specimen to have had its animal matter replaced by some mineral in order that it may be classed as a fossil, for the Siberian Mammoths, found entombed in ice, are very properly spoken of as fossils, although the flesh of at least one of these animals was so fresh that it was eaten. Likewise, the mammoth tusks brought to market are termed fossil-ivory, although differing but little from the tusks of modern elephants.

Many fossils indeed merit their popular appellation of petrifactions, because they have been changed into stone by the slow removal of the animal or vegetable matter present and its replacement by some mineral, usually silica or some form of lime. But it is necessary to include 'indications of plants or animals' in the above definition because some of the best fossils may be merely impressions of plants or animals and no portion of the objects themselves, and yet, as we shall see, some of our most important information has been gathered from these same imprints.

Nearly all our knowledge of the plants that flourished in the past is based on the impressions of their leaves left on the soft mud or smooth sand that later on hardened into enduring stone. Such, too, are the trails of creeping and crawling things, casts of the burrows of worms and the many footprints of the reptiles, great and small, that crept along the shore or stalked beside the waters of the ancient seas. The creatures themselves have passed away, their massive bones even are lost, but the prints of their feet are as plain to-day as when they were first made.

Many a crustacean, too, is known solely or mostly by the cast of its shell, the hard parts having completely vanished, and the existence of birds in some formations is revealed merely by the casts of their eggs; and these natural casts must be included in the category of fossils.

Impressions of vertebrates may, indeed, be almost as good as actual skeletons, as in the case of some fishes, where the fine mud in which they were buried has become changed to a rock, rivalling porcelain in texture; the bones have either dissolved away or shattered into dust at the splitting of the rock, but the imprint of each little fin-ray and every threadlike bone is as clearly defined as it would have been in a freshly prepared skeleton. So fine, indeed, may have been the mud, and so quiet for the time being the waters of the ancient sea or lake, that not only have prints of bones and leaves been found, but those of feathers and of the skin of some reptiles, and even of such soft and delicate objects as jelly fishes. But for these we should have little positive knowledge of the outward appearance of the creatures of the past, and to them we are occasionally indebted for the solution of some moot point in their anatomy.

The reader may possibly wonder why it is that fossils are not more abundant; why, of the vast majority of animals that have dwelt upon the earth since it became fit for the habitation of living beings, not a trace remains. This, too, when some objects—the tusks of the Mammoth, for example—have been sufficiently well preserved to form staple articles of commerce at the present time, so that the carved handle of my lady's parasol may have formed part of some animal that flourished at the very dawn of the human race, and been gazed upon by her grandfather a thousand times removed. The answer to this query is that, unless the conditions were such as to preserve at least the hard parts of any creature from immediate decay, there was small probability of it becoming fossilized. These conditions are that the objects must be protected from the air, and, practically, the only way that this happens in nature is by having them covered with water, or at least buried in wet ground.

13. Which of the following words (in bold) do **not** advance the writer's argument?
A. '**And** yet it is not essential for a specimen…'
B. '**Although** the flesh of at least one of these animals was so fresh that it was eaten…'
C. '**But** it is necessary to include…'
D. '**Yet**, as we shall see, some of our most important information…'
E. '**But** for these we should have little positive knowledge…'

14. How does the writer define 'fossils' in the first paragraph?
A. Remains, or even the indications, of animals and plants that have, through natural agencies, been buried in the earth and preserved for long periods of time
B. Remains of extinct animals or plants
C. Objects that have become petrified or turned into stone
D. All of the above
E. None of the above

15. Which of the following pair of words are **not** used as a direct comparison by the writer?
A. 'Animals' and 'plants'
B. 'Brief' and 'comprehensive'
C. 'Bones of the Great Auk and Rytina' and 'bones of many species of animals, still living'
D. 'Mammoth tusks' and 'tusks of modern elephants'
E. 'Soft mud or smooth sand' and 'enduring stone'

16. What does the writer believe is the answer to the question of why fossils are not more abundant?
A. They are difficult to discover
B. They require very specific conditions to form
C. They get destroyed easily
D. It is hard to define what a 'fossil' is
E. All of the above

5. Sanskrit

What, then, is it that gives to Sanskrit its claim on our attention, and its supreme importance in the eyes of the historian? First of all, its antiquity—for we know Sanskrit at an earlier period than Greek. But what is far more important than its merely chronological antiquity is the antique state of preservation in which that Aryan language has been handed down to us. The world had known Latin and Greek for centuries, and it was felt, no doubt, that there was some kind of similarity between the two. But how was that similarity to be explained? Sometimes Latin was supposed to give the key to the formation of a Greek word, sometimes Greek seemed to betray the secret of the origin of a Latin word. Afterward, when the ancient Teutonic languages, such as Gothic and Anglo-Saxon, and the ancient Celtic and Slavonic languages too, came to be studied, no one could help seeing a certain family likeness among them all. But how such a likeness between these languages came to be, and how, what is far more difficult to explain, such striking differences too between these languages came to be, remained a mystery, and gave rise to the most gratuitous theories, most of them, as you know, devoid of all scientific foundation. As soon, however, as Sanskrit stepped into the midst of these languages, there came light and warmth and mutual recognition. They all ceased to be strangers, and each fell of its own accord into its right place. Sanskrit was the eldest sister of them all, and could tell of many things which the other members of the family had quite forgotten. Still, the other languages too had each their own tale to tell; and it is out of all their tales together that a chapter in the human mind has been put together which, in some respects, is more important to us than any of the other chapters, the Jewish, the Greek, the Latin, or the Saxon. The process by which that ancient chapter of history was recovered is very simple. Take the words which occur in the same form and with the same meaning in all the seven branches of the Aryan family, and you have in them the most genuine and trustworthy records in which to read the thoughts of our true ancestors, before they had become Hindus, or Persians, or Greeks, or Romans, or Celts, or Teutons, or Slaves. Of course, some of these ancient charters may have been lost in one or other of these seven branches of the Aryan family, but even then, if they are found in six, or five, or four, or three, or even two only of its original branches, the probability remains, unless we can prove a later historical contact between these languages, that these words existed before the great Aryan Separation. If we find agni, meaning fire, in Sanskrit, and ignis, meaning fire, in Latin, we may safely conclude that fire was known to the undivided Aryans, even if no trace of the same name of fire occurred anywhere else. And why? Because there is no indication that Latin remained longer united with Sanskrit than any of the other Aryan languages, or that Latin could have borrowed such a word from Sanskrit, after these two languages had once become distinct. We have, however, the Lithuanian ugnìs, and the Scottish ingle, to show that the Slavonic and possibly the Teutonic languages also, knew the same word for fire, though they replaced it in time by other words. Words, like all other things, will die, and why they should live on in one soil and wither away and perish in another, is not always easy to say. What has become of ignis, for instance, in all the Romance languages? It has withered away and perished, probably because, after losing its final unaccentuated syllable, it became awkward to pronounce; and another word, focus, which in Latin meant fireplace, hearth, altar, has taken its place.

Suppose we wanted to know whether the ancient Aryans before their separation knew the mouse: we should only have to consult the principal Aryan dictionaries, and we should find in Sanskrit mûsh, in Greek μῦς, in Latin mus, in Old Slavonic mўse, in Old High German mûs, enabling us to say that, at a time so distant from us that we feel inclined to measure it by Indian rather than by our own chronology, the mouse was known, that is, was named, was conceived and recognized as a species of its own, not to be confounded with any other vermin. And if we were to ask whether the enemy of the mouse, the cat, was known at the same distant time, we should feel justified in saying decidedly, No. The cat is called in Sanskrit mârgâra and vidâla. In Greek and Latin the words usually given as names of the cat, γαλέη and αἴλουρος, mustella and feles, did not originally signify the tame cat, but the weasel or marten. The name for the real cat in Greek was κάττα, in Latin catus, and these words have supplied the names for cat in all the Teutonic, Slavonic, and Celtic languages. The animal itself, so far as we know at present, came to Europe from Egypt, where it had been worshipped for centuries and tamed; and as this arrival probably dates from the fourth century a.d., we can well understand that no common name for it could have existed when the Aryan nations separated. In this way a more or less complete picture of the state of civilization, previous to the Aryan Separation, can be and has been reconstructed, like a mosaic put together with the fragments of ancient stones; and I doubt whether, in tracing the history of the human mind, we shall ever reach to a lower stratum than that which is revealed to us by the converging rays of the different Aryan languages.

17. Which language does the writer state is the oldest?
A. Sanskrit
B. Greek
C. Latin
D. Gothic
E. Anglo-Saxon

18. Which of the following is **not** used as a metaphor?
A. Strangers
B. Eldest sister
C. Human mind
D. Mosaic
E. Fragments of ancient stone

19. The writer is of the view that:
A. We should only study Sanskrit and not Greek or Latin
B. Sanskrit helps us understand the relationship between the different ancient languages
C. Sanskrit is obsolete as it is the oldest language
D. Not enough attention is given to Sanskrit
E. None of the above

20. How does the writer suggest we understand the history of languages?
A. Consulting the dictionaries
B. Looking at the chronology
C. Comparing words which occur in the same form and same meaning
D. Looking at words like 'fire' or 'cat'
E. All of the above

6. Pre-adolescence

The years from about eight to twelve constitute a unique period of human life. The acute stage of teething is passing, the brain has acquired nearly its adult size and weight, health is almost at its best, activity is greater and more varied than it ever was before or ever will be again, and there is peculiar endurance, vitality, and resistance to fatigue. The child develops a life of its own outside the home circle, and its natural interests are never so independent of adult influence. Perception is very acute, and there is great immunity to exposure, danger, accident, as well as to temptation. Reason, true morality, religion, sympathy, love, and aesthetic enjoyment are but very slightly developed.

Everything, in short, suggests that this period may represent in the individual what was once for a very protracted and relatively stationary period an age of maturity in the remote ancestors of our race, when the young of our species, who were perhaps pygmoid, shifted for themselves independently of further parental aid. The qualities developed during pre-adolescence are, in the evolutionary history of the race, far older than hereditary traits of body and mind which develop later and which may be compared to a new and higher story built upon our primal nature. Heredity is so far both more stable and more secure. The elements of personality are few, but are well organised on a simple, effective plan. The momentum of these traits inherited from our indefinitely remote ancestors is great, and they are often clearly distinguishable from those to be added later. Thus the boy is father of the man in a new sense, in that his qualities are indefinitely older and existed, well compacted, untold ages before the more distinctly human attributes were developed. Indeed, there are a few faint indications of an earlier age node, at about the age of six, as if amid the instabilities of health, we could detect signs that this may have been the age of puberty in remote ages of the past. I have also given reasons that lead me to the conclusion that, despite its dominance, the function of sexual maturity and procreative power is peculiarly mobile up and down the age-line independently of many of the qualities usually so closely associated with it, so that much that sex created in the phylum now precedes it in the individual.

Rousseau would leave prepubescent years to nature and to these primal hereditary impulsions and allow the fundamental traits of savagery their fling till twelve. Biological psychology finds many and cogent reasons to confirm this view if only a proper environment could be provided. The child revels in savagery; and if its tribal, predatory, hunting, fishing, fighting, roving, idle, playing proclivities could be indulged in the country and under conditions that now, alas! seem hopelessly ideal, they could conceivably be so organized and directed as to be far more truly humanistic and liberal than all that the best modern school can provide. Rudimentary organs of the soul, now suppressed, perverted, or delayed, to crop out in menacing forms later, would be developed in their season so that we should be immune to them in maturer years, on the principle of the Aristotelian catharsis for which I have tried to suggest a far broader application than the Stagirite could see in his day.

These inborn and more or less savage instincts can and should be allowed some scope. The deep and strong cravings in the individual for those primitive experiences and occupations in which his ancestors became skilful through the pressure of necessity should not be ignored, but can and should be, at least partially, satisfied in a vicarious way, by tales from literature, history, and tradition which present the crude and primitive virtues of the heroes of the world's childhood. In this way, aided by his vivid visual imagination, the child may enter upon his heritage from the past, live out each stage of life to its fullest and realize in himself all its manifold tendencies. Echoes only of the vaster, richer life of the remote past of the race they must remain, but just these are the murmurings of the only muse that can save from the omnipresent dangers of precocity. Thus we not only rescue from the danger of loss, but utilize for further psychic growth the results of the higher heredity, which are the most precious and potential things on earth. So, too, in our urbanized hothouse life, that tends to ripen everything before its time, we must teach nature, although the very phrase is ominous. But we must not, in so doing, wean still more from, but perpetually incite to visit, field, forest, hill, shore, the water, flowers, animals, the true homes of childhood in this wild, undomesticated stage from which modern conditions have kidnapped and transported him. Books and reading are distasteful, for the very soul and body cry out for a more active, objective life, and to know nature and man at first hand. These two staples, stories and nature, by these informal methods of the home and the environment, constitute fundamental education.

21. The writer suggests that:
A. Children require more adult guidance
B. Children are able to be independent
C. Children should not read
D. Children should only play outside
E. Children need to be active outdoors on top of reading

22. Which of the following did the writer **not** suggest happens during years 8 to 12?
A. The start of teething
B. Growth in brain size
C. Improvement in health
D. Greater activity
E. Greater resistance to fatigue

23. Which of the following would the writer and Rosseau agree on?
A. Children should play outdoors more
B. Children should read
C. Children should be left to fend for themselves
D. Children should grow up in the wild
E. None of the above

24. Which sentence comes closest to the writer's views?
A. Reason, true morality, religion, sympathy, love, and aesthetic enjoyment are but very slightly developed
B. Heredity is so far both more stable and more secure
C. The boy is father of the man in a new sense, in that his qualities are indefinitely older and existed, well compacted, untold ages before the more distinctly human attributes were developed
D. The child revels in savagery; and if its tribal, predatory, hunting, fishing, fighting, roving, idle, playing proclivities could be indulged in the country and under conditions that now, alas! Seem hopelessly ideal
E. These two staples, stories and nature, by these informal methods of the home and the environment, constitute fundamental education

7. Life of Chopin

Deeply regretted as he may be by the whole body of artists, lamented by all who have ever known him, we must still be permitted to doubt if the time has even yet arrived in which he, whose loss is so peculiarly deplored by ourselves, can be appreciated in accordance with his just value, or occupy that high rank which in all probability will be assigned him in the future.

If it has been often proved that "no one is a prophet in his own country;" is it not equally true that the prophets, the men of the future, who feel its life in advance, and prefigure it in their works, are never recognized as prophets in their own times? It would be presumptuous to assert that it can ever be otherwise. In vain may the young generations of artists protest against the "Anti-progressives," whose invariable custom it is to assault and beat down the living with the dead: time alone can test the real value, or reveal the hidden beauties, either of musical compositions, or of kindred efforts in the sister arts.

As the manifold forms of art are but different incantations, charged with electricity from the soul of the artist, and destined to evoke the latent emotions and passions in order to render them sensible, intelligible, and, in some degree, tangible; so genius may be manifested in the invention of new forms, adapted, it may be, to the expression of feelings which have not yet surged within the limits of common experience, and are indeed first evoked within the magic circle by the creative power of artistic intuition. In arts in which sensation is linked to emotion, without the intermediate assistance of thought and reflection, the mere introduction of unaccustomed forms, of unused modes, must present an obstacle to the immediate comprehension of any very original composition. The surprise, nay, the fatigue, caused by the novelty of the singular impressions which it awakens, will make it appear to many as if written in a language of which they were ignorant, and which that reason will in itself be sufficient to induce them to pronounce a barbarous dialect. The trouble of accustoming the ear to it will repel many who will, in consequence, refuse to make a study of it. Through the more vivid and youthful organizations, less enthralled by the chains of habit; through the more ardent spirits, won first by curiosity, then filled with passion for the new idiom, must it penetrate and win the resisting and opposing public, which will finally catch the meaning, the aim, the construction, and at last render justice to its qualities, and acknowledge whatever beauty it may contain. Musicians who do not restrict themselves within the limits of conventional routine, have, consequently, more need than other artists of the aid of time. They cannot hope that death will bring that instantaneous plus-value to their works which it gives to those of the painters. No musician could renew, to the profit of his manuscripts, the deception practiced by one of the great Flemish painters, who, wishing in his lifetime to benefit by his future glory, directed his wife to spread abroad the news of his death, in order that the pictures with which he had taken care to cover the walls of his studio, might suddenly increase in value!

Whatever may be the present popularity of any part of the productions of one, broken, by suffering long before taken by death, it is nevertheless to be presumed that posterity will award to his works an estimation of a far higher character, of a much more earnest nature, than has hitherto been awarded them. A high rank must be assigned by the future historians of music to one who distinguished himself in art by a genius for melody so rare, by such graceful and remarkable enlargements of the harmonic tissue; and his triumph will be justly preferred to many of far more extended surface, though the works of such victors may be played and replayed by the greatest number of instruments, and be sung and resung by passing crowds of Prime Donne.

25. What point is the writer trying to make in the first paragraph?
A. Chopin died too young
B. It is doubtful whether Chopin should be appreciated
C. Chopin may be underrated
D. Chopin may be overrated
E. Chopin is too unknown

26. What is the writer's argument in the second paragraph?
A. A lifetime is insufficient to have notable achievements
B. Musicians tend to only be appreciated after they die
C. People focus too much on the living
D. A lifetime is insufficient to judge an artist's work
E. Dead musicians are always better than living musicians

27. Which of the following is **not** being used as a metaphor?
A. Electricity
B. Soul
C. Magic circle
D. Composition
E. Chains

28. The writer's main argument is that
A. Only death will increase a musician's value
B. We should focus more on living musicians than dead musicians
C. Young musicians need time for people to appreciate the work as people need to become accustomed to their unconventional music
D. Musicians should emulate the great Flemish painters
E. Musicians should not adopt unaccustomed forms or modes of composition

8. Religion and morality

It had been formerly asserted by theologians that our moral laws were given to man by a supernatural intuitive process. However, Professor E. A. Westermarck's "Origin and Development of the Moral Ideas," and similar researches, give a comprehensive survey of the moral ideas and practices of all the backward fragments of the human race and conclusively prove the social nature of moral law. The moral laws have evolved much the same as physical man has evolved. There is no indication whatsoever that the moral laws came from any revelation since the sense of moral law was just as strong amongst civilized peoples beyond the range of Christianity, or before the Christian era. Joseph McCabe, commenting on Professor Westermarck's work states, "All the fine theories of the philosophers break down before this vast collection of facts. There is no intuition whatever of an august and eternal law, and the less God is brought into connection with these pitiful blunders and often monstrous perversions of the moral sense, the better. What we see is just man's mind in possession of the idea that his conduct must be regulated by law, and clumsily working out the correct application of that idea as his intelligence grows and his social life becomes more complex. It is not a question of the mind of the savage imperfectly seeing the law. It is a plain case of the ideas of the savage reflecting and changing with his environment and the interest of his priests."

Justice is a fundamental and essential moral law because it is a vital regulation of social life and murder is the greatest crime because it is the greatest social delinquency; and these are inherent in the social nature of moral law. "Moral law slowly dawns in the mind of the human race as a regulation of a man's relation with his fellows in the interest of social life. It is quite independent of religion, since it has entirely different roots in human psychology." (Joseph McCabe: "Human Origin of Morals.")

In the mind of primitive man there is no connection between morality and the belief in a God. "Society is the school in which men learn to distinguish between right and wrong. The headmaster is custom and the lessons are the same for all. The first moral judgments were pronounced by public opinion; public indignation and public approval are the prototypes of the moral emotions." (Edward Westermarck: "Origin and Development of the Moral Ideas.")

Moral ideas and moral energy have their source in social life. It is only in a more advanced society that moral qualities are assumed for the gods. And indeed, it is known that in some primitive tribes, the gods are not necessarily conceived as good, they may have evil qualities also. "If they are, to his mind, good, that is so much the better. But whether they are good or bad they have to be faced as facts. The Gods, in short belong to the region of belief, while morality belongs to that of practice. It is in the nature of morality that it should be implicit in practice long before it is explicit in theory. Morality belongs to the group and is rooted in certain impulses that are a product of the essential conditions of group life. It is as reflection awakens that men are led to speculate upon the nature and origin of the moral feelings. Morality, whether in practice or theory, is thus based upon what is. On the other hand, religion, whether it be true or false, is in the nature of a discovery—one cannot conceive man actually ascribing ethical qualities to his Gods before he becomes sufficiently developed to formulate moral rules for his own guidance, and to create moral laws for his fellowmen. The moralization of the Gods will follow as a matter of course. Man really modifies his Gods in terms of the ideal human being. It is not the Gods who moralize man, it is man who moralizes the Gods." (Chapman Cohen: "Theism or Atheism.")

29. Which tone does the writer adopt?
A. Neutral
B. Investigative
C. Critical
D. Ironic
E. Sarcastic

30. Which philosopher mentioned in the passage disagrees with the viewpoint of the others?
A. Professor E. A. Westermarck
B. Joseph McCabe
C. Edward Westermarck
D. Chapman Cohen
E. They all agree with each other

31. Which sentence does not convey the same argument as the others?
A. Our moral laws were given to man by a supernatural intuitive process
B. Social nature of moral law
C. Moral law slowly dawns in the mind of the human race as a regulation of a man's relation with his fellows in the interest of social life
D. Moral ideas and moral energy have their source in social life
E. It is not the Gods who moralize man, it is man who moralizes the Gods

32. Which phrase is **not** used with a negative connotation in this passage?
A. Backward
B. Pitiful
C. Monstrous
D. Delinquency
E. Evil

9. Australia

To the people who lived four centuries ago in Europe only a very small portion of the earth's surface was known. Their geography was confined to the regions lying immediately around the Mediterranean, and including Europe, the north of Africa, and the west of Asia. Round these there was a margin, obscurely and imperfectly described in the reports of merchants; but by far the greater part of the world was utterly unknown. Great realms of darkness stretched all beyond, and closely hemmed in the little circle of light. In these unknown lands our ancestors loved to picture everything that was strange and mysterious. They believed that the man who could penetrate far enough would find countries where inexhaustible riches were to be gathered without toil from fertile shores, or marvellous valleys; and though wild tales were told of the dangers supposed to fill these regions, yet to the more daring and adventurous these only made the visions of boundless wealth and enchanting loveliness seem more fascinating.

Thus, as the art of navigation improved, and long voyages became possible, courageous seamen were tempted to venture out into the great unknown expanse. Columbus carried his trembling sailors over great tracts of unknown ocean, and discovered the two continents of America; Vasco di Gama penetrated far to the south, and rounded the Cape of Good Hope; Magellan, passing through the straits now called by his name, was the first to enter the Pacific Ocean; and so in the case of a hundred others, courage and skill carried the hardy seaman over many seas and into many lands that had lain unknown for ages.

Australia was the last part of the world to be thus visited and explored. In the year 1600, during the times of Shakespeare, the region to the south of the East Indies was still as little known as ever; the rude maps of those days had only a great blank where the islands of Australia should have been. Most people thought there was nothing but the ocean in that part of the world; and as the voyage was dangerous and very long—requiring several years for its completion—scarcely any one cared to run the risk of exploring it.

33. According to the passage, which region was the last to be explored?
A. Europe
B. Americas
C. North of Africa
D. West Asia
E. Australia

34. What was the reason why explorers were reluctant to explore Australia?
A. It was too expensive
B. There were not enough seamen
C. It was too risky
D. They did not think Australia existed
E. Navigation techniques were not good enough

35. Why did the explorers want to venture out further into the unknown?
A. They wanted to complete the map
B. They wanted passages named after them
C. Long navigation was possible
D. They believed they could get rich
E. They were seeking adventure

36. Which of the following was **not** a factor being the explorers being able to travel so far?
A. Money
B. Courage
C. Skills
D. Improvement in navigation
E. None of the above

10. Dreams

The subject which I have to discuss here is so complex, it raises so many questions of all kinds, difficult, obscure, some psychological, others physiological and metaphysical; in order to be treated in a complete manner it requires such a long development—and we have so little space, that I shall ask your permission to dispense with all preamble, to set aside un-essentials, and to go at once to the heart of the question.

A dream is this. I perceive objects and there is nothing there. I see men; I seem to speak to them and I hear what they answer; there is no one there and I have not spoken. It is all as if real things and real persons were there, then on waking all has disappeared, both persons and things. How does this happen?

But, first, is it true that there is nothing there? I mean, is there not presented a certain sense material to our eyes, to our ears, to our touch, etc., during sleep as well as during waking?

Close the eyes and look attentively at what goes on in the field of our vision. Many persons questioned on this point would say that nothing goes on, that they see nothing. No wonder at this, for a certain amount of practise is necessary to be able to observe oneself satisfactorily. But just give the requisite effort of attention, and you will distinguish, little by little, many things. First, in general, a black background. Upon this black background occasionally brilliant points which come and go, rising and descending, slowly and sedately. More often, spots of many colours, sometimes very dull, sometimes, on the contrary, with certain people, so brilliant that reality cannot compare with it. These spots spread and shrink, changing form and colour, constantly displacing one another. Sometimes the change is slow and gradual, sometimes again it is a whirlwind of vertiginous rapidity. Whence comes all this phantasmagoria? The physiologists and the psychologists have studied this play of colours. "Ocular spectra," "coloured spots," "phosphenes", such are the names that they have given to the phenomenon. They explain it either by the slight modifications which occur ceaselessly in the retinal circulation, or by the pressure that the closed lid exerts upon the eyeball, causing a mechanical excitation of the optic nerve. But the explanation of the phenomenon and the name that is given to it matters little. It occurs universally and it constitutes—I may say at once—the principal material of which we shape our dreams, "such stuff as dreams are made on."

37. What, according to the writer, is the 'heart of the question'?
A. What we see in dreams
B. What we hear in dreams
C. Our field of vision when we close our eyes
D. What are the 'play of colours'
E. What the physiologists and psychologists think

38. What does the writer think we see when we close our eyes?
A. Nothing
B. Perceived objects
C. Brilliant spots
D. Dull spots
E. There is no settled opinion

39. What does the writer agree with the physiologists and psychologists on?
A. We see colours when we close our eyes
B. The colours we see can be named 'ocular spectra', 'coloured spots' or 'phosphenes'
C. The phenomenon is due to slight modifications which occur ceaselessly in the retinal circulation
D. The phenomenon is due to pressure that the closed lid exerts upon the eyeball, causing a mechanical excitation of the optic nerve
E. None of the above

11. Pathological liars

The role played in society by the pathological liar is very striking. The characteristic behaviour in its unreasonableness is quite beyond the ken of the ordinary observer. The fact that here is a type of conduct regularly indulged in without seeming pleasurable results, and frequently militating obviously against the direct interests of the individual, makes a situation inexplicable by the usual canons of inference. To a certain extent the tendencies of each separate case must be viewed in their environmental context to be well understood. For example, the lying and swindling which centre about the assumption of a noble name and a corresponding station or affecting the life of a cloister brother, such as we find in the cases cited by Longard, show great differences from any material obtainable in our country. In interpretation of this, one has to consider the glamour thrown about the socially exalted or the life of the recluse—a glamour which obtains readily among the simple-minded people of rural Europe. Then, too, this very simple-mindedness, with the great differences which exist between peasant and noble, leads in itself to much opportunity for cheating.

With us, especially in the newer work of courts, which are rapidly becoming in their various social endeavours more and more intimately connected with many phases of life, the pathological liar becomes of main interest in the role of accuser of others, self-accuser, witness, and general social disturber.

Here again, we may call attention to the fact, which is of great social importance, namely, that the person who is seemingly normal in all other respects may be a pathological liar. It might be naturally expected that the feebleminded, who frequently have poor discernment of the relation of cause and effect, including the phenomena of conduct, would often lie without normal cause. As a matter of fact, there is surprisingly little of this among them, and one can find numerous mental defectives who are faithful tellers of the truth, while even, as we have found by other studies, some are good testifiers. Exaggerated instances of the type represented by Case 12, where the individual by the virtue of language ability endeavours to maintain a place in the world which his abilities do not otherwise justify, and where the very contradiction between abilities and disabilities leads to the development of an excessive habit of lying, are known in considerable number by us. Many of these mentally defective verbalists do not even grade high enough to come in our border-line cases, and yet frequently, by virtue of their gift of language, the world in general considers them fairly normal. They are really on a constant social strain by virtue of this, and while they are not purely pathological liars they often indulge in pathological lying, a distinction we have endeavoured to make clear in our introduction.

It stands out very clearly, both in previous studies of this subject and in viewing our own material, that pathological lying is very rarely the single offense of the pathological liar. The characteristics of this lying show that it arises from a tendency which might easily express itself in other forms of misrepresentation. Swindling, sometimes stealing, sometimes running away from home (assuming another character and perhaps another name) may be the results of the same general causes in the individual. The extent to which these other delinquencies are carried on by a pathological liar depends again largely upon environmental conditions—for instance, truancy is very difficult in German cities; a long career of thieving, under the better police surveillance of some European countries, is less possible than with us; while swindling, for the reason given above, seems easier there.

40. The writer is of the view that:
A. People can often tell who a pathological liar is
B. Pathological liars can easily integrate into society
C. Pathological liars often commit related offences
D. Pathological liars are good verbalists
E. Pathological liars are mentally-impaired

41. What does the writer want to show by using 'case 12'?
A. Pathological liars are often forced to lie
B. Pathological liars can easily integrate into society
C. Pathological liars lack the skills to contribute to society
D. Some pathological liars may be lying to fit into society
E. Pathological liars suffer from lying

42. What tone does the writer adopt?
A. Sarcastic
B. Critical
C. Analytical
D. One-sided
E. Ironic

END OF SECTION

YOU MUST ANSWER ONLY ONE OF THE FOLLOWING QUESTIONS

1. Is social media damaging for teenagers?

2. To what extent should journalists be responsible for 'fake news'?

3. Limitations should be put in place for scientific discovery. Discuss.

4. Too many students are going to University. Discuss

END OF TEST

THIS PAGE HAS BEEN

INTENTIONALLY LEFT BLANK

Mock Paper D

1. The fallacy of protection

All laws made for the purpose of protecting the interests of individuals or classes must mean, if they mean anything, to render the articles which such classes deal in or produce dearer than they would otherwise be if the public was left at liberty to supply itself with such commodities in the manner which their own interests and choice would dictate. In order to make them dearer it is absolutely necessary to make them scarcer; for quantity being large or small in proportion to demand, alone can regulate the price; —protection, therefore, to any commodity simply means that the quantity supplied to the community shall be less than circumstances would naturally provide, but that for the smaller quantity supplied under the restriction of law the same sum shall be paid as the larger quantity would command without such restriction.

Time was when the Sovereigns of England relied chiefly on the granting of patents to individuals for the exclusive exercise of certain trades or occupations in particular places, as the means of rewarding the services of some, and as a provision for others of their adherents, followers, and favourites, who either held the exclusive supply in their own hands on their own terms, or who again granted to others under them that privilege, receiving from them a portion of the gains. In the course of time, however, the public began to discover that these monopolies acted upon them directly as a tax of a most odious description; that the privileged person found it needful always to keep the supply short to obtain his high price (for as soon as he admitted plenty he had no command of price)—that, in short, the sovereign, in conferring a mark of regard on a favourite, gave not that which he himself possessed, but only invested him with the power of imposing a contribution on the public.

The public once awake to the true operation of such privileges, and severely suffering under the injuries which they inflicted, perseveringly struggled against these odious monopolies, until the system was entirely abandoned, and the crown was deprived of the power of granting patents of this class. But though the public saw clearly enough that these privileges granted by the sovereign to individuals operated thus prejudicially on the community, they did not see with equal clearness that the same power transferred to, and exercised by, Parliament, to confer similar privileges on classes; to do for a number of men what the sovereign had before done for single men, would, to the remaining portion of the community, be just as prejudicial as the abuses against which they had struggled. That like the sovereign, the Parliament, in protecting or giving privileges to a class, gave nothing which they possessed themselves, but granted only the power to such classes of raising a contribution from the remaining portion of the community, by levying a higher price for their commodity than it would otherwise command. As with individuals, it was equally necessary to make scarcity to secure price, and that could only be done by restricting the sources of supply by prohibiting, or by imposing high duties on, foreign importations. Many circumstances, however, combined to render the use of this power by Parliament less obvious than it had been when exercised by the sovereign, but chiefly the fact that protection was usually granted by imposing high duties, often in their effect quite prohibitory, under the plea of providing revenue for the state. Many other more modern excuses have been urged, such as those of encouraging native industry, and countervailing peculiar burthens, in order to reconcile public opinion to the exactions arising out of the system, all of which we shall, on future occasions, carefully consider separately. But, above all, the great reason why these evils have been so long endured has been, that the public have believed that all classes and interests, though perhaps not exactly to the same extent, have shared in protection. We propose at present to confine our consideration to the effects of protection, —first, on the community generally; and secondly, on the individual classes protected.

1. The writer takes the view that:
A. Laws were implemented for the benefit of the public
B. Laws were implied indiscriminately
C. The public did not have a say in the laws being implemented
D. Only certain classes of people benefited from the laws at the expense of the rest of the public
E. None of the above

2. The writer suggests in the first paragraph that:
A. Laws are meant for protecting the interests of individuals or classes
B. Commodities should remain scarce
C. Laws result in the price of commodities being increased
D. Laws cannot affect the demand and supply of commodities
E. All of the above

3. According to the second paragraph, what was the original intention behind patents?
A. Exclusive exercise of certain trades or occupations in particular places
B. Taxation
C. Keep the supply short
D. Increase prices
E. None of the above

4. With regards to the imposition of high duties, which reasoning would the writer agree with?
A. Providing revenue for the state
B. Encouraging native industry
C. Countervailing peculiar burthens
D. All of the above
E. None of the above

2. Camouflage

The art of concealment or camouflage is one of the newest and most highly developed techniques of modern warfare. But the animals have been masters of it for ages. The lives of most of them are passed in constant conflict. Those which have enemies from which they cannot escape by rapidity of motion must be able to hide or disguise themselves. Those which hunt for a living must be able to approach their prey without unnecessary noise or attention to themselves. It is very remarkable how Nature helps the wild creatures to disguise themselves by colouring them with various shades and tints best calculated to enable them to escape enemies or to entrap prey.

The animals of each locality are usually coloured according to their habitat, but good reasons make some exceptions advisable. Many of the most striking examples of this protective resemblance among animals are the result of their very intimate association with the surrounding flora and natural scenery. There is no part of a tree, including flowers, fruits, bark and roots, that is not in some way copied and imitated by these clever creatures. Often this imitation is astonishing in its faithfulness of detail. Bunches of cocoanuts are portrayed by sleeping monkeys, while even the leaves are copied by certain tree-toads, and many flowers are represented by monkeys and lizards. The winding roots of huge trees are copied by snakes that twist themselves together at the foot of the tree.

In the art of camouflage—an art which affects the form, colour, and attitude of animals—Nature has worked along two different roads. One is easy and direct, the other circuitous and difficult. The easy way is that of protective resemblance pure and simple, where the animal's colour, form, or attitude becomes like that of its habitat. In which case the animal becomes one with its environment and thus is enabled to go about unnoticed by its enemies or by its prey. The other way is that of bluff, and it includes all inoffensive animals which are capable of assuming attitudes and colours that terrify and frighten. The colours in some cases are really of warning pattern, yet they cannot be considered mimetic unless they are thought to resemble the patterns of some extinct model of which we know nothing; and since they are not found in present-day animals with unpleasant qualities, they are not, strictly speaking, warning colours.

Desert animals are in most cases desert-coloured. The lion, for example, is almost invisible when crouched among the rocks and streams of the African wastes. Antelopes are tinted like the landscape over which they roam, while the camel seems actually to blend with the desert sands. The kangaroos of Australia at a little distance seem to disappear into the soil of their respective localities, while the cat of the Pampas accurately reflects his surroundings in his fur.

The tiger is made so invisible by his wonderful colour that, when he crouches in the bright sunlight amid the tall brown grass, it is almost impossible to see him. But the zebra and the giraffe are the kings of all camouflagers! So deceptive are the large blotch-spots of the giraffe and his weird head and horns, like scrubby limbs, that his concealment is perfect. Even the cleverest natives often mistake a herd of giraffes for a clump of trees. The camouflage of zebras is equally deceptive. Drummond says that he once found himself in a forest, looking at what he thought to be a lone zebra, when to his astonishment he suddenly realised that he was facing an entire herd which were invisible until they became frightened and moved. Evidently the zebra is well aware that the black-and-white stripes of his coat take away the sense of solid body, and that the two colours blend into a light grey, and thus at close range the effect is that of rays of sunlight passing through bushes.

5. Which of the following is **not** a reason put forward by the writer behind the purpose of camouflage for animals?
A. Modern warfare
B. Hide or disguise themselves from enemies
C. Approach their prey without unnecessary noise or attention to themselves
D. All of the above
E. None of the above

6. 'Nature has worked along two different roads' – what are the two different roads mentioned by the writer?
A. Two different ways of camouflage
B. Two different functions of camouflage
C. Two levels of complexity behind camouflage
D. None of the above
E. All of the above

7. Which animal mentioned below has a distinctively different method of camouflage from the others?
A. Desert animals
B. Tiger
C. Zebra
D. Giraffe
E. They all adopt similar methods

8. What tone does the writer adopt throughout the passage?
A. Ironic
B. Sarcastic
C. Analytic
D. Critical
E. Inquisitive

3. History of Nature

We live in and form part of a system of things of immense diversity and perplexity, which we call Nature; and it is a matter of the deepest interest to all of us that we should form just conceptions of the constitution of that system and of its past history. With relation to this universe, man is, in extent, little more than a mathematical point; in duration but a fleeting shadow; he is a mere reed shaken in the winds of force. But as Pascal long ago remarked, although a mere reed, he is a thinking reed; and in virtue of that wonderful capacity of thought, he has the power of framing for himself a symbolic conception of the universe, which, although doubtless highly imperfect and inadequate as a picture of the great whole, is yet sufficient to serve him as a chart for the guidance of his practical affairs. It has taken long ages of toilsome and often fruitless labour to enable man to look steadily at the shifting scenes of the phantasmagoria of Nature, to notice what is fixed among her fluctuations, and what is regular among her apparent irregularities; and it is only comparatively lately, within the last few centuries, that the conception of a universal order and of a definite course of things, which we term the course of Nature, has emerged.

But, once originated, the conception of the constancy of the order of Nature has become the dominant idea of modern thought. To any person who is familiar with the facts upon which that conception is based, and is competent to estimate their significance, it has ceased to be conceivable that chance should have any place in the universe, or that events should depend upon any but the natural sequence of cause and effect. We have come to look upon the present as the child of the past and as the parent of the future; and, as we have excluded chance from a place in the universe, so we ignore, even as a possibility, the notion of any interference with the order of Nature. Whatever may be men's speculative doctrines, it is quite certain that every intelligent person guides his life and risks his fortune upon the belief that the order of Nature is constant, and that the chain of natural causation is never broken.

In fact, no belief which we entertain has so complete a logical basis as that to which I have just referred. It tacitly underlies every process of reasoning; it is the foundation of every act of the will. It is based upon the broadest induction, and it is verified by the most constant, regular, and universal of deductive processes. But we must recollect that any human belief, however broad its basis, however defensible it may seem, is, after all, only a probable belief, and that our widest and safest generalisations are simply statements of the highest degree of probability. Though we are quite clear about the constancy of the order of Nature, at the present time, and in the present state of things, it by no means necessarily follows that we are justified in expanding this generalisation into the infinite past, and in denying, absolutely, that there may have been a time when Nature did not follow a fixed order, when the relations of cause and effect were not definite, and when extra-natural agencies interfered with the general course of Nature. Cautious men will allow that a universe so different from that which we know may have existed; just as a very candid thinker may admit that a world in which two and two do not make four, and in which two straight lines do enclose a space, may exist. But the same caution which forces the admission of such possibilities demands a great deal of evidence before it recognises them to be anything more substantial. And when it is asserted that, so many thousand years ago, events occurred in a manner utterly foreign to and inconsistent with the existing laws of Nature, men, who without being particularly cautious, are simply honest thinkers, unwilling to deceive themselves or delude others, ask for trustworthy evidence of the fact.

9. Why does the writer capitalise the word 'Nature'?
A. To emphasise its importance
B. The writer is not using the word in its natural meaning
C. To refer to 'nature' as an entity
D. The writer is using it as a name
E. The writer think it is customary to capitalise the word 'Nature'

10. Which of the following is **not** used as a metaphor?
A. Universe
B. Mathematical point
C. Shadow
D. Reed
E. None of the above

11. Which of the following is presented as a fact rather than an opinion?
A. 'We live in and form part of a system of things of immense diversity and perplexity'
B. 'But as Pascal long ago remarked, although a mere reed, he is a thinking reed'
C. 'Whatever may be men's speculative doctrines, it is quite certain that every intelligent person guides his life and risks his fortune upon the belief that the order of Nature is constant, and that the chain of natural causation is never broken'
D. 'In fact, no belief which we entertain has so complete a logical basis as that to which I have just referred'
E. 'But we must recollect that any human belief, however broad its basis, however defensible it may seem, is, after all, only a probable belief'

12. Which of the following statements would the author most agree with?
A. Men are always capable of understanding Nature
B. Men can only estimate to the highest probability what they understand about Nature
C. Nature cannot be understood as it is too complex
D. Men are not intelligent enough to understand Nature
E. Men are too insignificant in Nature

4. The selection theory

In artificial selection the breeder chooses out for pairing only such individuals as possess the character desired by him in a somewhat higher degree than the rest of the race. Some of the descendants inherit this character, often in a still higher degree, and if this method be pursued throughout several generations, the race is transformed in respect of that particular character.

Natural selection depends on the same three factors as artificial selection: on variability, inheritance, and selection for breeding, but this last is here carried out not by a breeder but by what Darwin called the "struggle for existence." This last factor is one of the special features of the Darwinian conception of nature. That there are carnivorous animals which take heavy toll in every generation of the progeny of the animals on which they prey, and that there are herbivores which decimate the plants in every generation had long been known, but it is only since Darwin's time that sufficient attention has been paid to the facts that, in addition to this regular destruction, there exists between the members of a species a keen competition for space and food, which limits multiplication, and that numerous individuals of each species perish because of unfavourable climatic conditions. The "struggle for existence," which Darwin regarded as taking the place of the human breeder in free nature, is not a direct struggle between carnivores and their prey, but is the assumed competition for survival between individuals of the same species, of which, on an average, only those survive to reproduce which have the greatest power of resistance, while the others, less favourably constituted, perish early. This struggle is so keen, that, within a limited area, where the conditions of life have long remained unchanged, of every species, whatever be the degree of fertility, only two, on an average, of the descendants of each pair survive; the others succumb either to enemies, or to disadvantages of climate, or to accident. A high degree of fertility is thus not an indication of the special success of a species, but of the numerous dangers that have attended its evolution. Of the six young brought forth by a pair of elephants in the course of their lives only two survive in a given area; similarly, of the millions of eggs which two thread-worms leave behind them only two survive. It is thus possible to estimate the dangers which threaten a species by its ratio of elimination, or, since this cannot be done directly, by its fertility.

Although a great number of the descendants of each generation fall victims to accident, among those that remain it is still the greater or less fitness of the organism that determines the "selection for breeding purposes," and it would be incomprehensible if, in this competition, it was not ultimately, that is, on an average, the best equipped which survive, in the sense of living long enough to reproduce.

Thus the principle of natural selection is the selection of the best for reproduction, whether the "best" refers to the whole constitution, to one or more parts of the organism, or to one or more stages of development. Every organ, every part, every character of an animal, fertility and intelligence included, must be improved in this manner, and be gradually brought up in the course of generations to its highest attainable state of perfection. And not only may improvement of parts be brought about in this way, but new parts and organs may arise, since, through the slow and minute steps of individual or "fluctuating" variations, a part may be added here or dropped out there, and thus something new is produced.

13. Which of the following is a difference between artificial selection and natural selection?
A. Variability
B. Inheritance
C. Selection for breeding
D. None of the above
E. All of the above

14. What contributes to the 'struggle for existence'?
A. Carnivorous animals which take heavy toll in every generation of the progeny of the animals on which they prey
B. Herbivores which decimate the plants in every generation
C. Keen competition for space and food
D. Unfavourable climatic conditions
E. All of the above

15. 'Thus the principle of natural selection is the selection of the best for reproduction' – which of the following does not fall under the writer's definition of 'best'?
A. Organs of an animal
B. Fitness of an animal
C. Avoiding accidents
D. Fertility
E. Intelligence

16. Which of the following is **not** an example of natural selection?
A. The breeder chooses out for pairing only such individuals as possess the character desired by him in a somewhat higher degree than the rest of the race
B. Keen competition for space and food which limits multiplication
C. Numerous individuals of each species perish because of unfavourable climatic conditions
D. Of every species, whatever be the degree of fertility, only two, on an average, of the descendants of each pair survive
E. The others succumb either to enemies, or to disadvantages of climate, or to accident

5. Heredity

One of the best attested single characters in human heredity is brachydactyly, "short-fingerness," which results in a reduction in the length of the fingers by the dropping out of one joint. If one lumps together all the cases where any effect of this sort is found, it is evident that normals never transmit it to their posterity, that affected persons always do, and that in a mating between a normal and an affected person, all the offspring will show the abnormality. It is a good example of a unit character.

But its effect is by no means confined to the fingers. It tends to affect the entire skeleton, and in a family where one child is markedly brachydactylous, that child is generally shorter than the others. The factor for brachydactyly evidently produces its primary effect on the bones of the hand, but it also produces a secondary effect on all the bones of the body.

Moreover, it will be found, if a number of brachydactylous persons are examined, that no two of them are affected to exactly the same degree. In some cases, only one finger will be abnormal; in other cases there will be a slight effect in all the fingers; in other cases all the fingers will be highly affected. Why is there such variation in the results produced by a unit character? Because, presumably, in each individual there is a different set of modifying factors or else a variation in the factor. It has been found that an abnormality quite like brachydactyly is produced by abnormality in the pituitary gland. It is then fair to suppose that the factor which produces brachydactyly does so by affecting the pituitary gland in some way. But there must be many other factors which also affect the pituitary and in some cases probably favour its development, rather than hindering it. Then if the factor for brachydactyly is depressing the pituitary, but if some other factors are at the same time stimulating that gland, the effect shown in the subject's fingers will be much less marked than if a group of modifying factors were present which acted in the same direction as the brachydactyly factor, —to perturb the action of the pituitary gland.

This illustration is largely hypothetical; but there is no room for doubt that every factor produces more than a single effect. A white blaze in the hair, for example, is a well-proved unit factor in man; the factor not only produces a white streak in the hair, but affects the pigmentation of the skin as well, usually resulting in one or more white spots on some part of the body. It is really a factor for "piebaldism."

For the sake of clear thinking, then, the idea of a unit character due to some unit determiner or factor in the germ-plasm must be given up, and it must be recognized that every visible character of an individual is the result of numerous factors, or differences in the germ-plasm. Ordinarily one of these produces a more notable contribution to the end-product than do the others; but there are cases where this statement does not appear to hold good. This leads to the conception of multiple factors.

17. Which of the following is not a possible side-effect of brachydactyly?
A. Reduction in the length of one finger
B. Reduction in the length of all fingers
C. Decrease in height
D. Dropping out of one joint
E. All of the above

18. Based on the information provided in the passage, which set of parents will **not** produce an offspring with brachydactyly?
A. Two normal parents
B. Two affected parents
C. One affected parent and one normal parent
D. A and B only
E. None of the above

19. What explanation does the writer provide for the difference in seriousness of the brachydactyly in affected individuals?
A. Individuals that are more affected have two parents who were affected
B. Individuals that are more affected have only one parent who was affected
C. The more affected individuals had a weak constitution to begin with
D. The more affected individuals had other factors that contributed to the seriousness of the brachydactyly
E. These individuals have weak pituitary glands

20. What is the writer's overall conclusion?
A. The genes determining brachydactyly are solely responsible for producing short fingers
B. Different traits of a person are the result of numerous factors
C. One affected parent is enough for a child to be affected with the illness
D. Brachydactyly and piebaldism are similar
E. Brachydactyly and piebaldism have wide-ranging effects on the body

6. Buddhism in China

Buddhism was not an indigenous religion of China. Its founder was Gautama of India in the sixth century B.C. Some centuries later it found its way into China by way of central Asia. There is a tradition that as early as 142 B.C. Chang Ch'ien, an ambassador of the Chinese emperor, Wu Ti, visited the countries of central Asia, where he first learned about the new religion which was making such headway and reported concerning it to his master. A few years later the generals of Wu Ti captured a gold image of the Buddha which the emperor set up in his palace and worshiped, but he took no further steps.

According to Chinese historians' Buddhism was officially recognized in China about 67 A.D. A few years before that date, the emperor, Ming-Ti, saw in a dream a large golden image with a halo hovering above his palace. His advisers, some of whom were no doubt already favourable to the new religion, interpreted the image of the dream to be that of Buddha, the great sage of India, who was inviting his adhesion. Following their advice the emperor sent an embassy to study into Buddhism. It brought back two Indian monks and a quantity of Buddhist classics. These were carried on a white horse and so the monastery which the emperor built for the monks and those who came after them was called the White Horse Monastery. Its tablet is said to have survived to this day.

This dream story is worth repeating because it goes to show that Buddhism was not only known at an early date, but was favoured at the court of China. In fact, the same history which relates the dream contains the biography of an official who became an adherent of Buddhism a few years before the dream took place. This is not at all surprising, because an acquaintance with Buddhism was the inevitable concomitant of the military campaigning, the many embassies and the wide-ranging trade of those centuries. But the introduction of Buddhism into China was especially promoted by reason of the current policy of the Chinese government of moving conquered populations in countries west of China into China proper, the vanquished peoples brought their own religion along with them. At one time what is now the province of Shansi was populated in this way by the Hsiung-nu, many of whom were Buddhists.

The introduction and spread of Buddhism were hastened by the decline of Confucianism and Taoism. The Han dynasty (206 B. C.-221 A. D.) established a government founded on Confucianism. It reproduced the classics destroyed in the previous dynasty and encouraged their study; it established the state worship of Confucius; it based its laws and regulations upon the ideals and principles advocated by Confucius. The great increase of wealth and power under this dynasty led to a gradual deterioration in the character of the rulers and officials. The rigid Confucian regulations became burdensome to the people who ceased to respect their leaders. Confucianism lost its hold as the complete solution of the problems of life. At the same time Taoism had become a veritable jumble of meaningless and superstitious rites which served to support a horde of ignorant, selfish priests. The high religious ideals of the earlier Taoist mystics were abandoned for a search after the elixir of life during fruitless journeys to the isles of the Immortals which were supposed to be in the Eastern Sea.

21. According to the writer, Buddhism originated in:
A. India
B. China
C. Central Asia
D. West of China
E. Shansi

22. Which of the following is **not** a reason given for the rise of Buddhism in China?
A. The generals of Wu Ti captured a gold image of the Buddha which the emperor set up in his palace and worshiped
B. The emperor sent an embassy to study into Buddhism
C. Buddhism was favoured at the court of China
D. Decline of Confucianism and Taoism
E. None of the above

23. Which of the following is a reason why Confucianism started to decline?
A. The Han Dynasty established the state worship of Confucius
B. The Han Dynasty based its laws and regulations upon the ideals and principles advocated by Confucius
C. The great increase of wealth and power under the Han Dynasty
D. Gradual deterioration in the character of the rulers and officials
E. All of the above

24. What is the writer's purpose behind introducing the 'dream story'?
A. Showing how superstitious the Chinese were
B. The exact date of the introduction of Buddhism was disputed
C. The introduction of Buddhism had questionable origins
D. Buddhism was introduced at an early date
E. Buddhism was not introduced because of the decline of Confucianism and Taoism

7. Science in England

That the state of knowledge in any country will exert a directive influence on the general system of instruction adopted in it, is a principle too obvious to require investigation. And it is equally certain that the tastes and pursuits of our manhood will bear on them the traces of the earlier impressions of our education. It is therefore not unreasonable to suppose that some portion of the neglect of science in England, may be attributed to the system of education we pursue. A young man passes from our public schools to the universities, ignorant almost of the elements of every branch of useful knowledge; and at these latter establishments, formed originally for instructing those who are intended for the clerical profession, classical and mathematical pursuits are nearly the sole objects proposed to the student's ambition.

Much has been done at one of our universities during the last fifteen years, to improve the system of study; and I am confident that there is no one connected with that body, who will not do me the justice to believe that, whatever suggestions I may venture to offer, are prompted by the warmest feelings for the honour and the increasing prosperity of its institutions. The ties which connect me with Cambridge are indeed of no ordinary kind.

Taking it then for granted that our system of academical education ought to be adapted to nearly the whole of the aristocracy of the country, I am inclined to believe that whilst the modifications I should propose would not be great innovations on the spirit of our institutions, they would contribute materially to that important object.

It will be readily admitted, that a degree conferred by an university, ought to be a pledge to the public that he who holds it possesses a certain quantity of knowledge. The progress of society has rendered knowledge far more various in its kinds than it used to be; and to meet this variety in the tastes and inclinations of those who come to us for instruction, we have, besides the regular lectures to which all must attend, other sources of information from whence the students may acquire sound and varied knowledge in the numerous lectures on chemistry, geology, botany, history, etc. It is at present a matter of option with the student, which, and how many of these courses he shall attend, and such it should still remain. All that it would be necessary to add would be, that previously to taking his degree, each person should be examined by those Professors, whose lectures he had attended. The pupils should then be arranged in two classes, according to their merits, and the names included in these classes should be printed. I would then propose that no young man, except his name was found amongst the "List of Honours", should be allowed to take his degree, unless he had been placed in the first class of someone at least of the courses given by the professors. But it should still be imperative upon the student to possess such mathematical knowledge as we usually require. If he had attained the first rank in several of these examinations, it is obvious that we should run no hazard in a little relaxing: the strictness of his mathematical trial.

25. Which of the following is presented as a **fact** by the writer?

A. That the state of knowledge in any country will exert a directive influence on the general system of instruction adopted in it, is a principle too obvious to require investigation

B. And it is equally certain that the tastes and pursuits of our manhood will bear on them the traces of the earlier impressions of our education

C. Much has been done at one of our universities during the last fifteen years, to improve the system of study

D. I am confident that there is no one connected with that body, who will not do me the justice to believe that, whatever suggestions I may venture to offer, are prompted by the warmest feelings for the honour and the increasing prosperity of its institutions

E. The ties which connect me with Cambridge are indeed of no ordinary kind

26. Who is the passage addressed to?

A. Students

B. Professors

C. Universities

D. Scientists

E. Young people

27. What is the writer's main argument?

A. Students are graded too leniently

B. The clerical profession, classical and mathematical pursuits are the sole objects of education

C. Students do not know enough about science

D. Students should aspire to get a First Class Honours

E. Universities are not providing good education

28. What tone does the writer adopt in this passage?

A. Analytical

B. Critical

C. Sarcastic

D. Ironic

E. Neutral

8. Women's suffrage

The prolonged slavery of woman is the darkest page in human history. A survey of the condition of the race through those barbarous periods, when physical force governed the world, when the motto, "might makes right," was the law, enables one to account, for the origin of woman's subjection to man without referring the fact to the general inferiority of the sex, or Nature's law.

Writers on this question differ as to the cause of the universal degradation of woman in all periods and nations.

One of the greatest minds of the century has thrown a ray of light on this gloomy picture by tracing the origin of woman's slavery to the same principle of selfishness and love of power in man that has thus far dominated all weaker nations and classes. This brings hope of final emancipation, for as all nations and classes are gradually, one after another, asserting and maintaining their independence, the path is clear for woman to follow. The slavish instinct of an oppressed class has led her to toil patiently through the ages, giving all and asking little, cheerfully sharing with man all perils and privations by land and sea, that husband and sons might attain honour and success. Justice and freedom for herself is her latest and highest demand.

Another writer asserts that the tyranny of man over woman has its roots, after all, in his nobler feelings; his love, his chivalry, and his desire to protect woman in the barbarous periods of pillage, lust, and war. But wherever the roots may be traced, the results at this hour are equally disastrous to woman. Her best interests and happiness do not seem to have been consulted in the arrangements made for her protection. She has been bought and sold, caressed and crucified at the will and pleasure of her master. But if a chivalrous desire to protect woman has always been the mainspring of man's dominion over her, it should have prompted him to place in her hands the same weapons of defence he has found to be most effective against wrong and oppression.

It is often asserted that as woman has always been man's slave—subject—inferior—dependent, under all forms of government and religion, slavery must be her normal condition. This might have some weight had not the vast majority of men also been enslaved for centuries to kings and popes, and orders of nobility, who, in the progress of civilization, have reached complete equality. And did we not also see the great changes in woman's condition, the marvellous transformation in her character, from a toy in the Turkish harem, or a drudge in the German fields, to a leader of thought in the literary circles of France, England, and America!

In an age when the wrongs of society are adjusted in the courts and at the ballot-box, material force yields to reason and majorities.

Woman's steady march onward, and her growing desire for a broader outlook, prove that she has not reached her normal condition, and that society has not yet conceded all that is necessary for its attainment.

29. Which of the following is presented as a **fact**?
A. The prolonged slavery of woman is the darkest page in human history
B. A survey of the condition of the race through those barbarous periods, when physical force governed the world, when the motto, "might makes right," was the law, enables one to account, for the origin of woman's subjection to man without referring the fact to the general inferiority of the sex, or Nature's law
C. Writers on this question differ as to the cause of the universal degradation of woman in all periods and nations
D. The slavish instinct of an oppressed class has led her to toil patiently through the ages, giving all and asking little
E. Justice and freedom for herself is her latest and highest demand

30. Which word is **not** being used with a negative connotation?
A. Darkest
B. Barbarous
C. Inferiority
D. Gloomy
E. None of the above

31. Which tone does the writer adopt?
A. Inquisitive
B. Sceptical
C. Critical
D. Opinionated
E. Factual

32. What is the writer's overall argument?
A. Women are unable to acquire better rights than men
B. Women are constantly oppressed
C. Women are still in the journey of fighting for the rights they deserve
D. Men have a tendency to harm women instead of protecting them
E. Men can also be oppressed

9. Christianity and Islam

A comparison of Christianity with Muhammedanism or with any other religion must be preceded by a statement of the objects with which such comparison is undertaken, for the possibilities which lie in this direction are numerous. The missionary, for instance, may consider that a knowledge of the similarities of these religions would increase the efficacy of his proselytising work: his purpose would thus be wholly practical. The ecclesiastically minded Christian, already convinced of the superiority of his own religion, will be chiefly anxious to secure scientific proof of the fact: the study of comparative religion from this point of view was once a popular branch of apologetics and is by no means out of favour at the present day. Again, the inquirer whose historical perspective is undisturbed by ecclesiastical considerations, will approach the subject with somewhat different interests. He will expect the comparison to provide him with a clear view of the influence which Christianity has exerted upon other religions or has itself received from them: or he may hope by comparing the general development of special religious systems to gain a clearer insight into the growth of Christianity. Hence the object of such comparisons is to trace the course of analogous developments and the interaction of influence and so to increase the knowledge of religion in general or of our own religion in particular.

A world-religion, such as Christianity, is a highly complex structure and the evolution of such a system of belief is best understood by examining a religion to which we have not been bound by a thousand ties from the earliest days of our lives. If we take an alien religion as our subject of investigation, we shall not shrink from the consequences of the historical method: whereas, when we criticise Christianity, we are often unable to see the falsity of the pre-suppositions which we necessarily bring to the task of inquiry: our minds follow the doctrines of Christianity, even as our bodies perform their functions—in complete unconsciousness. At the same time, we possess a very considerable knowledge of the development of Christianity, and this we owe largely to the help of analogy. Especially instructive is the comparison between Christianity and Buddhism. No less interesting are the discoveries to be attained by an inquiry into the development of Muhammedanism: here we can see the growth of tradition proceeding in the full light of historical criticism. We see the plain man, Muhammed, expressly declaring in the Qoran that he cannot perform miracles, yet gradually becoming a miracle worker and indeed the greatest of his class: he professes to be nothing more than a mortal man: he becomes the chief mediator between man and God. The scanty memorials of the man become voluminous biographies of the saint and increase from generation to generation.

Yet more remarkable is the fact that his utterances, his logia, if we may use the term, some few of which are certainly genuine, increase from year to year and form a large collection which is critically sifted and expounded. The aspirations of mankind attribute to him such words of the New Testament and of Greek philosophers as were especially popular or seemed worthy of Muhammed; the teaching also of the new ecclesiastical schools was invariably expressed in the form of proverbial utterances attributed to Muhammed, and these are now without exception regarded as authentic by the modern Moslem. In this way opinions often contradictory are covered by Muhummed's authority.

33. What does the writer think is the purpose of a comparison of religions?
A. Increase the efficacy of proselytising work
B. Secure scientific proof to determine the superiority of a religion
C. Provide a clear view of the of religions upon each other
D. Gain a clearer insight into the growth of a religion
E. None of the above

34. What is the writer's views with regards to Muhammedanism?
A. It is inferior to Christianity
B. It is similar to Buddhism
C. It criticises Christianity
D. It helps us view Christianity more critically
E. It is similar to Christianity

35. Who is more likely to **not** have a biased opinion towards their religion according to the passage?
A. Missionaries
B. Ecclesiastically-minded Christian
C. Inquirer whose historical perspective is undisturbed by ecclesiastical considerations
D. Muhammed
E. Greek philosophers

36. The writer argues in the second paragraph that:
A. Christians are blinded by their religion
B. Muhammedanism provides a false comparison to Christianity
C. We need to compare Christianity to similar religions
D. We need to compare Christianity to dissimilar religions
E. Muhammedanism is critical of Christianity

10. Yeast

I have selected tonight the particular subject of yeast for two reasons—or, rather, I should say for three. In the first place, because it is one of the simplest and the most familiar objects with which we are acquainted. In the second place, because the facts and phenomena which I have to describe are so simple that it is possible to put them before you without the help of any of those pictures or diagrams which are needed when matters are more complicated, and which, if I had to refer to them here, would involve the necessity of my turning away from you now and then, and thereby increasing very largely my difficulty (already sufficiently great) in making myself heard. And thirdly, I have chosen this subject because I know of no familiar substance forming part of our every-day knowledge and experience, the examination of which, with a little care, tends to open up such very considerable issues as does this substance—yeast.

In the first place, I should like to call your attention to a fact with which the whole of you are, to begin with, perfectly acquainted, I mean the fact that any liquid containing sugar, any liquid which is formed by pressing out the succulent parts of the fruits of plants, or a mixture of honey and water, if left to itself for a short time, begins to undergo a peculiar change. No matter how clear it might be at starting, yet after a few hours, or at most a few days, if the temperature is high, this liquid begins to be turbid, and by-and-by bubbles make their appearance in it, and a sort of dirty-looking yellowish foam or scum collects at the surface; while at the same time, by degrees, a similar kind of matter, which we call the "lees," sinks to the bottom.

The quantity of this dirty-looking stuff, that we call the scum and the lees, goes on increasing until it reaches a certain amount, and then it stops; and by the time it stops, you find the liquid in which this matter has been formed has become altered in its quality. To begin with it was a mere sweetish substance, having the flavour of whatever might be the plant from which it was expressed, or having merely the taste and the absence of smell of a solution of sugar; but by the time that this change that I have been briefly describing to you is accomplished the liquid has become completely altered, it has acquired a peculiar smell, and, what is still more remarkable, it has gained the property of intoxicating the person who drinks it. Nothing can be more innocent than a solution of sugar; nothing can be less innocent, if taken in excess, as you all know, than those fermented matters which are produced from sugar. Well, again, if you notice that bubbling, or, as it were, seething of the liquid, which has accompanied the whole of this process, you will find that it is produced by the evolution of little bubbles of air-like substance out of the liquid; and I dare say you all know this air-like substance is not like common air; it is not a substance which a man can breathe with impunity. You often hear of accidents which take place in brewers' vats when men go in carelessly, and get suffocated there without knowing that there was anything evil awaiting them. And if you tried the experiment with this liquid I am telling of while it was fermenting, you would find that any small animal let down into the vessel would be similarly stifled; and you would discover that a light lowered down into it would go out. Well, then, lastly, if after this liquid has been thus altered you expose it to that process which is called distillation; that is to say, if you put it into a still, and collect the matters which are sent over, you obtain, when you first heat it, a clear transparent liquid, which, however, is something totally different from water; it is much lighter; it has a strong smell, and it has an acrid taste; and it possesses the same intoxicating power as the original liquid, but in a much more intense degree. If you put a light to it, it burns with a bright flame, and it is that substance which we know as spirits of wine.

37. Which of the following is **not** a reason why the writer chose yeast as a topic for discussion?
A. It is one of the simplest and the most familiar objects with which we are acquainted
B. The facts and phenomena are simple
C. Pictures or diagrams can be used
D. It forms our every-day knowledge and experience
E. There are considerable issues to be discussed

38. Which of the following is **not** used to describe the formation of yeast?
A. Succulent
B. Turbid
C. Dirty-looking
D. Yellowish
E. Peculiar

39. Which of the following pair of words is **not** being used as a comparison?
A. 'Facts' and 'phenomena'
B. 'Clear' and 'turbid'
C. 'Sweetish' and 'peculiar'
D. 'Innocent' and 'intoxicating'
E. 'Clear' and 'intense'

11. Falling in love

Falling in Love, as modern biology teaches us to believe, is nothing more than the latest, highest, and most involved exemplification, in the human race, of that almost universal selective process which Mr. Darwin has enabled us to recognise throughout the whole long series of the animal kingdom. The butterfly that circles and eddies in his aërial dance around his observant mate is endeavouring to charm her by the delicacy of his colouring, and to overcome her coyness by the display of his skill. The peacock that struts about in imperial pride under the eyes of his attentive hens, is really contributing to the future beauty and strength of his race by collecting to himself a harem through whom he hands down to posterity the valuable qualities which have gained the admiration of his mates in his own person. Mr. Wallace has shown that to be beautiful is to be efficient; and sexual selection is thus, as it were, a mere lateral form of natural selection—a survival of the fittest in the guise of mutual attractiveness and mutual adaptability, producing on the average a maximum of the best properties of the race in the resulting offspring. I need not dwell here upon this aspect of the case, because it is one with which, since the publication of the 'Descent of Man,' all the world has been sufficiently familiar.

In our own species, the selective process is marked by all the features common to selection throughout the whole animal kingdom; but it is also, as might be expected, far more specialised, far more individualised, far more cognisant of personal traits and minor peculiarities. It is furthermore exerted to a far greater extent upon mental and moral as well as physical peculiarities in the individual.

We cannot fall in love with everybody alike. Some of us fall in love with one person, some with another. This instinctive and deep-seated differential feeling we may regard as the outcome of complementary features, mental, moral, or physical, in the two persons concerned; and experience shows us that, in nine cases out of ten, it is a reciprocal affection, that is to say, in other words, an affection roused in unison by varying qualities in the respective individuals.

Of its eminently conservative and even upward tendency very little doubt can be reasonably entertained. We do fall in love, taking us in the lump, with the young, the beautiful, the strong, and the healthy; we do not fall in love, taking us in the lump, with the aged, the ugly, the feeble, and the sickly. The prohibition of the Church is scarcely needed to prevent a man from marrying his grandmother. Moralists have always borne a special grudge to pretty faces; but, as Mr. Herbert Spencer admirably put it (long before the appearance of Darwin's selective theory), 'the saying that beauty is but skin-deep is itself but a skin-deep saying.' In reality, beauty is one of the very best guides we can possibly have to the desirability, so far as race-preservation is concerned, of any man or any woman as a partner in marriage. A fine form, a good figure, a beautiful bust, a round arm and neck, a fresh complexion, a lovely face, are all outward and visible signs of the physical qualities that on the whole conspire to make up a healthy and vigorous wife and mother; they imply soundness, fertility, a good circulation, a good digestion. Conversely, sallowness and paleness are roughly indicative of dyspepsia and anæmia; a flat chest is a symptom of deficient maternity; and what we call a bad figure is really, in one way or another, an unhealthy departure from the central norma and standard of the race. Good teeth mean good deglutition; a clear eye means an active liver; scrubbiness and undersizedness mean feeble virility. Nor are indications of mental and moral efficiency by any means wanting as recognised elements in personal beauty. A good-humoured face is in itself almost pretty. A pleasant smile half redeems unattractive features. Low, receding foreheads strike us unfavourably. Heavy, stolid, half-idiotic countenances can never be beautiful, however regular their lines and contours. Intelligence and goodness are almost as necessary as health and vigour in order to make up our perfect ideal of a beautiful human face and figure. The Apollo Belvedere is no fool; the murderers in the Chamber of Horrors at Madame Tussaud's are for the most part no beauties.

40. The writer uses the examples of the butterfly and peacock to illustrate:
A. Modern biologists' theory of Falling in Love
B. Darwin's theory
C. The fallacy of A and B
D. The workings of A and B
E. The differences between men and animals

41. According to the writer, which of the following is **not** a difference between love in mankind compared to the animal kingdom?
A. Degree of specialisation
B. Degree of individualisation
C. Cognisance of personal traits
D. Cognisance of minor peculiarities
E. All of the above

42. 'The saying that beauty is but skin-deep is itself but a skin-deep saying.' – what does the writer mean by this?
A. Only good-looking people find love
B. A natural attraction towards good-looking people is in line with the selection theory
C. It is superficial to focus on looks
D. Looks do not last
E. Good-looking people tend to be healthier

END OF SECTION

YOU MUST ANSWER ONLY ONE OF THE FOLLOWING QUESTIONS

1. Should the voting age be reduced?

2. Should tuition fees be reduced?

3. Tourism does more harm than good. Discuss.

4. Banning the wearing of a headscarf in the public sector is discriminatory. Discuss.

END OF SECTION

ANSWERS

Answer Key

Paper A		Paper B		Paper C		Paper D	
1	C	1	B	1	C	1	D
2	D	2	E	2	D	2	C
3	B	3	C	3	A	3	A
4	C	4	D	4	A	4	E
5	A	5	A	5	E	5	A
6	D	6	B	6	D	6	E
7	E	7	B	7	B	7	E
8	A	8	D	8	C	8	C
9	A	9	E	9	E	9	C
10	B	10	B	10	C	10	A
11	E	11	C	11	C	11	A
12	C	12	D	12	A	12	B
13	B	13	A	13	B	13	C
14	D	14	D	14	A	14	E
15	E	15	B	15	A	15	C
16	A	16	C	16	B	16	A
17	C	17	A	17	A	17	D
18	C	18	D	18	C	18	A
19	B	19	B	19	B	19	D
20	D	20	C	20	C	20	B
21	E	21	A	21	E	21	A
22	D	22	B	22	A	22	A
23	A	23	D	23	A	23	D
24	E	24	D	24	E	24	D
25	E	25	E	25	C	25	C
26	E	26	C	26	B	26	C
27	A	27	B	27	D	27	C
28	C	28	A	28	C	28	B
29	B	29	B	29	C	29	C
30	D	30	A	30	E	30	E
31	B	31	E	31	A	31	D
32	A	32	D	32	A	32	C
33	B	33	C	33	E	33	E
34	E	34	A	34	C	34	D
35	C	35	C	35	D	35	C
36	A	36	D	36	A	36	D
37	E	37	B	37	D	37	C
38	D	38	A	38	E	38	A
39	C	39	B	39	A	39	A
40	E	40	E	40	C	40	D
41	B	41	C	41	D	41	E
42	C	42	A	42	C	42	B

Mock Paper Answers

Mock Paper A: Section A

Extract 1

1. C is the correct answer. A is not incorrect, but is not the purpose of the comparison. B is about the importance of universality, not efficiency. D is not particularly relevant. E is correct, but it is more of a *conclusion* of the author, not the purpose behind the comparison
2. D is the correct answer. A is overtly mentioned in the first sentence. B is not really relevant to the piece, there is no implication that the younger generation will change their gaming habits on the basis of efficiency. C is explicitly mentioned in the sentence beginning 'Now, one…'. D is almost certainly correct, but is still an assumption which leads to the assertion in the first paragraph. E is irrelevant.
3. B is the correct answer. A is incorrect as it appears to be a rhetorical question. B Is most likely to be correct, as it draws parallels between the choice that the younger generation make on a day to day basis, and the choice that they often do not think about. By bringing them into the same sentence, he makes them seem equal. C is not correct, as although he does mention that younger people have lots of choices to make, he does not imply that this is overwhelming. D is correct, but the question is placed there in the context of the paragraph, which is clearly to do with other choices to be made. E, again, might be correct, but is not the reason he concludes the third paragraph in that way.

Extract 2

4. C is the correct answer. Although the statement says that the researchers 'propose', it is a statement of fact that this is what the researchers propose.
5. A is the correct answer. The author mentions that even though it may not help academically, it can help create a human being with good habits. This, along with the author's tendency to consider homework in a positive light implies that good habits and personality is as important as academics. B is stated outright. C, although may be inferred, is not necessarily implied by the author in the first sentence. D seems a little too far-fetched. It could be implied that busy work is not as important as other work, but it's too much of a leap to assume that she meant to imply that these teachers are *failing* their students. E, again is a step too far. It is clear form the piece that she does not agree with Kohn's work, but to conclude that it is untrustworthy would be incorrect.
6. D is the correct answer. This question refers to the second sentence of the last paragraph. A assumes that earning money is the equivalent of success. B refers to the child's mindset, which is not the same as 'methods'. C is a direct quotation from earlier in the extract, but this is not asserted as something that a child *needs*, instead it is stated as an inevitable result of children doing homework. E is irrelevant.
7. E is the correct answer. This question will be between C and E. C, however is too black and white, saying that homework is *not* helpful for academic achievement, where the article is less direct on that issue.

Extract 3

8. A is the correct answer. Although B is stated explicitly in the text, it is not the reason *why* the author uses the example, instead it is a question that is raised as a result of the use of the example. C cannot be correct as the author cannot emphasise a point that he has not yet made. D is incorrect, not only for the purpose of the example, but the piece altogether, as is E.
9. A is the correct answer. This is simply a question of close textual interpretation. A is identical to the first sentence of the last paragraph. B states that they are entirely different concepts, therefore not linked, which is not true. C is not true, as although the last sentence states that they must be *viewed* in the same way, the identities themselves are clearly not identical. D is not really dealt with at all, and E is not dealt with in the final paragraph (and is an incorrect interpretation of what was said previously)
10. B is the correct answer. B is taking a statement too far. The extract only suggests that the theory of tolerance is 'yet to be tested', not that tolerance has failed. A and C are stated in the piece (with different words). D is implied by the phrase beginning 'whatever else 'Britishness' might be'. E is implied with the brackets '(as we might be of 'Englishness' if we looked close enough)'.

Extract 4

11. 11. E is the correct answer. All of the statements could be a valid reason why the author has included the reference to certain airlines.
12. 12. C is the correct answer. This may well be a method used by retailers, but is not mentioned outright in the article. A is mentioned in relation to furniture shops. B is 'drip pricing'. D is the 'BOGOF' offers. E is in relation to the paragraph about 'price discrimination over time'
13. B is the correct answer. This question is about very close interpretation of the structure of the question. There is a difference between 'Why is it suggested that "people are not as rational as the standard economic model implies"?' and 'Why is it suggested that people are not as rational as the standard economic model implies?'. The use of a quotation in the first example implies that the question is asking why the author suggests something, or why the author uses a particular piece of evidence. However, the second structure is really asking 'Why are people not as rational as the standard economic market implies'. The inclusion of the 'is it suggested that' is only to remind the reader that the following part of the sentence is only a suggestion by Heuristics, it is not fact. Thus, the students may get confused between A and B. C is another example of the incorrect analysis of the question. D is incorrect as it is too strong a conclusion to draw. E is simply incorrect.
14. D is the correct answer. This will likely be a choice between A and D. Although the last paragraph lists some advice for consumers, this seems almost an odd addition to end the extract with. The purpose of the main extract, excluding this section, seems to be to inform the reader about the different methods used. Thus, overall, the extract seems to be informative, rather than advisory. The last paragraph is simply an addition on how to best make use of the information gained from the piece. C is also focusing on the 'advisory' last paragraph instead of the meaning of the piece as a whole. E is a homage to the title of the piece, but is not really relevant to the content.

Extract 5

15. E is the correct answer. A is stated. B is not an assumption. It may be implied by the author, or inferred by the reader, but an assumption is something that must be true in order for the author's argument to make sense. B does not fulfil this criterion. C, again might be implied by the author, especially for subjects that he considered irrelevant (namely homeopathy in this instance), but it is not rightly an 'assumption'. D is not relevant to the discussion of university as an investment. E is the correct answer, as, for the author's argument about university being an investment to be correct, he must admit that there are no other reasons why someone could want to go. If he admits that they are other reasons, then his argument is fatally flawed.
16. A is the correct answer. A is explicitly stated at the beginning of the penultimate paragraph. B is only correct in relation to non-Russell Group universities. C is incorrect, as the author only implies that university is too expensive for certain degrees. For D, the author never goes so far as to suggest that the degree is worthless, he just suggests that it is not worth the fees. E is incorrect, as the author suggests only that Russell Group universities are worth attending. This extends further than Oxbridge.
17. C is the correct answer. The author describes how university is beneficial for some people but not for others, his approach to this suggests that he believes the system is flawed. A is clearly an accurate description of the author's views of some parts of the university system, but not others. B is the option which may cause the most confusion for students. Whilst the passage does not seem to be supportive of the university system, it does make clear that there are certain universities that are beneficial to their attendees. Thus it is a step too far to argue that the author is not supportive of all aspects of the university system. D, again is too far in the opposite direction. The author, despite arguing that some aspects of the system are overpriced and unhelpful, does not conclude that the system as a whole is completely useless. E is clearly wrong.

Extract 6

18. C is the correct answer. A is pretty much irrelevant, but for the fact that money for arts could be going on emergency services, but this is a weak argument. B would strengthen the author's argument. For E, correlation does not necessarily mean causation and thus is not as strong as it would seem. C and D could both potentially weaken the author's argument, but C is more damaging to the author's perspective.
19. B is the correct answer. The use of the word 'desperate' indicates the author's aversion to Ms Miller. A is not the author's opinion, it is a direct quote from Richard Morrison. C is not about the author's distaste for Ms Miller but a description of the quote that he has just used. D is clearly positive. E does not show any opinion either way, it is merely a statement of fact.
20. D is the correct answer. A is stated at the beginning of paragraph 4. B is stated in the sentence 'The knives appear to be out for her in government'. C is stated in the first paragraph. E is clear. D is the answer as, even though the article states that 'much of the effect of the cut might be ameliorated through the National Lottery', it does not go so far as to state that it will make up the whole of the 5% cut in the arts.
21. E is the correct answer. A is incorrect as the question is not whether they are currently widely accepted. B is the option that the students are most likely to get confused with. This is very slightly wrong, as the question is not whether the arts are more worthy than they once were (although this is mentioned earlier), the question is whether they should be get 'special treatment'. Furthermore, it is not about being 'widely accepted' it is about whether local authorities will accept the idea. C is not really relevant - there is no mention of different opinions. The 4th answer is a moral question -should it be considered a special case, instead of whether it will be considered a special case.

Extract 7

22. D is the correct answer. A is mentioned in the observation that 'almost all respondents grew up in a male-dominated household'. B is explicitly mentioned in that 96% of respondents were male. C is mentioned in the penultimate paragraph.
23. A is the correct answer. B is causally related, as shown in the penultimate paragraph. C is mentioned in the exploration of the respondents' male-dominated households. D a relatively obvious point shown in the first sentence of the second paragraph. E is more subtle, with reference to people being 'pushed over the edge' in response to 'all Muslims [being] treated as terrorists'. A is the only one that is not causally related, there is no mention that the domination of extremism in the media has led to more extremism.
24. E is the correct answer. A and B are both mentioned in the extract, but neither is mentioned as being 'the definitive reason'. C is not even mentioned in the extract (though it may be inferred). D seems to be correct, as none of the above are 'the definitive reason'. However, choosing this option would admit that there is, in fact, one definitive reason. This is incorrect, as the author does not, at any point state that one correlation is more important than any of the others.
25. E is the correct answer. A is mentioned in the main body of the text, but is not the conclusion of the final two paragraphs. B is not mentioned at all, so is clearly wrong. C and D are mentioned in the penultimate paragraph, but are only part of the conclusion, not the main conclusion.

Extract 8

26. E is the correct answer. A is incorrect, but is likely to be picked by students. The growth of online pharmacies is not the reason why the misuse of medicine is becoming more of a topic. If anything, the growth of online pharmacies has led to medicine becoming more readily available which has in turn made it more of an issue. However, there is a missing link in the analysis to say that the growth of online pharmacies had led to a large issue of misuse of medicine. For example, the growth of online pharmacies could conceivably make it less of an issue, as it could make it more difficult for people to get medicine - perhaps because it's more difficult to prove to a computer that you deserve the medicine. B, too, is not directly responsible for the rise in relevance of misuse of medicines, it is only a factor. C and D may be inferred from the first paragraph, but it is not suggested. E is directly mentioned by the Chairman.
27. A is the correct answer. A is implied by Prof. Iversen in his 'Cat and mouse' analogy, where he states that the cat 'should not withdraw in defeat'. B and D are stated explicitly and thus cannot be said to have been implied. C is implied, but not by Prof. Iversen. Though both academics discuss pregabalin, it is only Professor Hill who mentions anything to do with the drug's widespread use. E is simply incorrect.

28. C is the correct answer. This question has been added to see if the students can determine whether a new person is being referred to, or simply more information is given about an already present character in the story. For example, the first paragraph refers to 'the government's senior drug adviser' and the second to 'Professor Les Iversen', where these are in fact the same person. The correct answer is C, the three people being Professor Iversen, the Home Secretary and Professor Hill.

Extract 9

29. B is the correct answer. A is incorrect - the argument relies on the premise that late-term abortions are legal, not that they have recently become legalised. B is correct, as the author simply assumes that mothers have the choice to terminate the pregnancy - this statement relies on the assumption that mothers alone are legally able to make this decision. C is incorrect - the author suggests that it may be more positive to wait until a child is born to decide whether or not to terminate its life, as there will be certainty that the child has no chance of survival. This would lead to more cases of infant euthanasia, but the reason they have increased in frequency is development in ultrasound scans such that spina bifida can be detected before birth. D is explicitly stated in the description of the illness as 'lethal'. E is a difficult one - the author may be implying this, by stating that it is 'not necessarily the best course of action', or indeed the reader might have inferred it, but it is not quite correct to state that the author assumed it in his argument - an assumption is an assertion of a fact or set on facts upon which an argument is based . This is not quite the case here.
30. D is the correct answer. In this case, incorrect students will most likely pick E, as it is the least controversial statement and thus most likely to be right. But the author does more than simply state that more discussion should be had. Throughout the article he mainly suggests positive things about a narrow legalisation of the euthanasia of children, both explicitly and implicitly, by favouring the arguments and countries that have accepted it. Further, in the conclusory paragraph he states 'parents, physicians, hospitals and nation need to confront this issue'. This is one step further than simply 'discussing': the use of the word 'confront' implies that they should decide positively on the benefits of legalisation and make changes.
31. B is the correct answer. Proof of parents supporting child euthanasia suggests that even parents, whose natural instincts are to care for their children, agree that in certain circumstances child euthanasia is beneficial. Both A and D suggest that spina bifida is a bad disease, which would support the view that late-term abortion is preferential to child euthanasia and thus sit against the author's stance. A significant rise in child mortality rate, as suggested with C is also detrimental to the author's cause. At first glance E may seem to be positive, as it looks like the President of the EU supports the author's plight, but upon further inspection, the President does not actually support the legalisation of child euthanasia, but merely stated that it should be explored more. This, in itself, does not support the author's argument.
32. A is the correct answer. A is the most likely of the correct answers. B may well be true, but it does not explain why the author began with that particular sentence. C may well be true of the first paragraph, as a push (though it seems more likely that the paragraph is included to shock the reader), but not of the first sentence, as this does not inform of the methods used, merely that they are easy. D is incorrect as both A and B could be possible reasons: E is incorrect as C is not a possibility.

Extract 10

33. B is the correct answer. This is a 'process of elimination' type question - A is not the 'ultimate aim', it is simply the method used. C is merely an intermediate step towards meeting the ultimate aim. D is incorrect, as the article does not suggest that this method can be used to stop any other disease except for Dengue Fever. E is irrelevant. Therefore, it must be B.
34. E is the correct answer. This question is likely to be a toss-up between A and E. Both B and C basically conclude that the project will not work, but this is not terrible, as it doesn't have any negative impact, it only reduces the potential positive impact. D shows that the evidence might be wrong, but this is not as bad as it definitely being wrong. The problem that arises between A and E is that, whilst one (A) is only a potential problem, if it were to arise the consequence would be worse, whereas (E) is a definite problem, but the consequence is not as bad as would arise if A came to fruition. On balance, though, the most damning statement should be E, as the fact that it is definitely transmittable is more damning, especially given that the consequence (infertility) remains quite serious. If for example, E were 'The discovery that Wolbachia can be transmitted to, and causes the sniffles in, humans', then on balance A would be more damning.

35. C is the correct answer. A is addressed in the reference to 'transparency and proper information for the households'. This implies that without such information, people may panic. B and E are directly addressed in the phrase ending 'concerns at the time that Wolbachia could infect humans and domestic animals'. D is less obvious, but arises from the fact that the author reassures the reader that, using this process, researchers will not have to 'constantly release more contaminated insects'. This suggests that, were the process not as adequate, this may have been a problem. C is the correct answer because, though the 10 week period is mentioned in relation to the experiment in Australia, there is no suggestion that taking longer than this would be problematic.

Extract 11

36. A is the correct answer. For A, the 'word seriously' is mean as a descriptive word about how affected the women's liberation movement is. B brings with it images of people putting their two cents into an argument- 'weighing in' usually carries with it negative connotations. C is pretty clearly negative, with the use of the word 'sacrifice' immediately bringing negativity with it. For D, the use of 'the sort of men' again carries with it less than friendly implications. E's use of the description 'hot pink', which tends to be associated with air-headedness for the word 'equivocation' suggests that she does not believe that it is.
37. E is the correct answer. Although some of the reasons identified are more prominent than others (for example, explaining what the fonts are like is probably not the main reason that Laurie Penny uses the word) all of them are possible reasons.
38. D is the correct answer. The answer most likely to be considered sarcastic is C. However, this is not sarcasm in the true sense of the word. Sarcasm occurs when someone says the opposite of what they mean in order to draw attention to it. The archetypal example being a grumpy teenager moaning 'oh great' in response to being made to do something that they don't want to do. C is not an example of sarcasm. It is factitious and full of attitude, but is not rightly categorised as sarcastic. More accurately it would be described as litotes – understatement for comic effect.
39. C is the correct answer. A is found in the idea that feminists want to change the may people think - they 'ask men to embrace a world where they do not get extra treats. B is mentioned in the discussion of why you cannot simply 'rebrand' feminism. D is implied by the paragraph beginning 'It is not "young women today" who need to be convinced that feminism remains necessary and "relevant". E is explicitly stated: 'the ugly, unfuckable feminist'. C, on the other hand is used to describe women, specifically how the magazines want women to be - it is not directly related to feminism as a concept

Extract 12

40. E is the correct answer. A is clearly wrong. B, C and D are all possible interpretations of what he's said, but his main opinion is E, as he mentions the implications for further study three times.
41. B is the correct answer. A is incorrect as the dust is simply the 'petri dish' of the experiment, the surface upon which the chemical reactions take place. C is correct in that it is radioactive, but there is no mention of it being an atom. D is clearly incorrect as the first paragraph notes that Iso-propyl cyanide is 'closer to' complex organic molecules. This by its very nature means that it is not the same thing. E is incorrect as it is only 'a step closer to discovering [...] the precursors ... of amino acids.'
42. C is the correct answer. A and D are incorrect as they are stated explicitly. B is incorrect as it is not about amino acids. E is incorrect as it is never mentioned that amino acids are essential, but only a possible way to explore life outside of earth. C can be inferred by joining together the ideas that Iso-propyl cyanide is radioactive, and that Iso-propyl cyanide could be the 'origin of more complex branched molecules, such as amino acids'

END OF SECTION

Mock Paper A: Section B

1. “The government should legalise the sale of human organs” Discuss.

For

- Bring it out of the black market
- Make it safer
- Could ensure that there are certain forms, stamps etc. to make sure that a good price is being paid, the person is consenting etc.
- Stop the need for human trafficking
- Bodily autonomy
    - People should be allowed to do whatever they want with their body
    - We allow this when we are *donating* organs - why not allow it into the capitalist system - it is proven to deal best with supply and demand issues
- Will allow desperate people a final option
    - Is it not better to sell organs than sell your body or descend into a life of crime

Against

- Why should we allow rich people with the means to pay to be able to buy organs to prolong their life, where other people may not be able to
- Is it *right* for life itself to be part of a capitalised system
- Perhaps we already do this? Allow rich people access to more experimental and expensive medicine - perhaps the question should be more about whether all humans should have access to the same medical treatment?
- Is it *right* to sell organs - should it not remain a donation based system - is making it a commodity the best way to deal with the issue of not having enough organs? Perhaps an ‘opt-out’ rather than ‘opt in’ system would create the supply required without needed to address the moral issue of whether one should be able to sell bits of themselves.
- Do we want desperate people to have to resort to selling their own organs?
    - Legalising it may make it an option for people, where it may not have been before

2. “Developed countries have a higher obligation to combat climate change than developing countries” Discuss the extent to which you agree with this statement.

For

- Higher GDP - more ‘disposable income’
- Moral obligation - MEDCs have benefitted from the earth’s resources more than other countries, so have more of an obligation to make it better
- MEDCs have the technology and capacity to develop new systems to prevent/slow down climate change
- LEDC’s have more important things on their mind
    - See ‘pyramid of needs’ below - those in MEDCs have already dealt with the bottom layer, so they can deal with the second layer.
    - Those in LEDC’s cannot deal with the red layer until the yellow layer is secured

Against

- Do they have a higher *moral* obligation? Perhaps it is true that practically the MEDC’s should be targeting climate change more aggressively than LEDC’s, but maybe this is because they have more resources to do it, it is not a matter of morality
- We know that one of the main causes of methane in the atmosphere is agriculture - cows mainly. These are more likely to be found in less developed countries. Thus, logic would suggest that these countries are equally responsible, if not more so than more developed countries
- It is not disputed that MEDCs should do more, but it is not because of *morals*
- It’s a universal problem - it faces everyone, so should be deal with by everyone

3. '"Putin is a serious threat to global stability" Discuss.

For

- It is a rarity in this day and age for a country to simply decide that they want land back, and just go in to take it
- His intention is ultimately to undermine democracy - he is a traditional 'baddie' - power hungry
- He cannot be defeated by manpower. He is not a 'extremist organisation which can be bombed. He is in a position of power, and thus has a unique position to undermine *global* security. He is a permanent threat
- He cannot be defeated by manpower. He is not a 'extremist organisation which can be bombed. He is in a position of power, and thus has a unique position to undermine *global* security. He is a permanent threat.
- Having such a strong, power hungry person in charge of such an extensive nuclear arsenal could result in a new cold war.

Against

- Need to explore whether this means Putin as a person, or Russia. How much power does Putin as a person really have, in the grand scheme of things?
- People have been scared of Russia as a concept since the cold war
- Its perceived character makes Putin seem more intimidating than other, similar people
- Is it Putin himself that is causing a threat to global stability, or the world's reaction to his actions
- We need an enemy, and if it weren't Putin, it would be someone else
- The media needs a target - and politicians follow - e.g. - The Ukraine problem got 'boring', so the media moved onto Islamic state
- How often do we hear about the Ukraine now? And has the problem actually ended?

4. "Sufferers of anorexia nervosa should be force fed" Do you agree with this statement? If so, evaluate at what point of an individual's disease this measure should be taken.

For

- This is a question about consent to medical treatment - As a result of thumb we do not treat people unless they consent to the treatment. Sufferers of anorexia nervosa who do not want to eat clearly do not consent to being fed. However, there are situations when we let this happen, if someone is considered too mentally ill to be able to give a free and informed consent.
- Anorexia is a disease whose physical symptoms all stem from the person not eating. Often the only way to save someone's life is to give them food. If they do not consent, it is indicative of the fact that they are incapable of logical thought, and the state should step in to help them, despite the intrusion on their bodily autonomy.
- There is no other option - they need food, they won't eat it.

Against

- Bodily autonomy - anorexia is not a mental illness like other mental illnesses - they still have their faculties and should be able to refuse treatment - even if this results in death
- Force-feeding is a humiliating, horrendous thing to have to go through (it has been used as a form of torture). There must be better ways of keeping someone alive until the disease releases its grip
- Could the humiliation of being force-fed aggravate the mental disorder?

END OF PAPER

Mock Paper B: Section A

Extract 1

1. B is the correct answer. Firstly we can discount E. A cannot be correct as the government cannot have implied anything specific about Egypt and Sudan, as these countries are not mentioned. C is too strong a sentiment to have been implied from what is a fairly neutral statement. D is most likely to be correct, but the statement cannot stretch so far as to have implied this. They only admit to having 'redressed' the balance. This cannot be taken to mean 'retaliation'. B is correct as the government states outright that Ethiopia was left bereft of access to the Nile, which suggests that they were overlooked in the past.

2. E is the correct answer. A can be discounted outright. Both C and D show passion, but do not go so far as show disdain. B is merely a statement of fact and does not suggest how the people of Ethiopia feel. E is correct as the use of the strong 'nefarious' suggests an underlying feeling of distaste.

3. C is the correct answer. The question asks why the particular phrase is used. All of the other answers refer to the context in which the phrase is used (the building of the Dam) and do not focus on the phrase itself. B and D might confuse some students, but it must be remembered that it is not asked what Mr Hossam's argument is, nor why he chose to explain that sentiment, but why he chose to use exaggeration within that particular phrase.

Extract 2

4. D is the correct answer. C can be discounted immediately. A and B are both conclusions reached in the article but are not the *main* conclusion of the article. E is a conclusion that might be inferred from what the author has said throughout, but is not stated within the article and thus it would be a stretch to say that it is the main conclusion. The article keeps returning to the idea of the healthy robbing the ill of their choice to i.e. - this must factor in the main conclusion of the article and so the answer must be D.
5. A is the correct answer. C and D are expressly stated in the article so there is no room to infer them. B is not even alluded to, so to infer something so extreme would be illogical. E is touched upon in the piece, however, the author states that his work regarding those who wish to die with dignity should be commended, so clearly he is rightly placed to discuss *some* aspects of the laws. The correct inference here comes from the statement 'the fact remains that he is a rich, powerful man and it is highly unlikely that his wishes would be ignored'. A logical inference here would be that others who aren't in his position might not be afforded the same luxury.

6. B is the correct answer. A will not support the author's argument as she clearly says that some people's opinion of what they think they will want if they become ill may change if and when they find themselves in that situation. C may rectify the problem that the author identifies with regards to the choices of the rich and famous being respected above the choices of the vulnerable, but this is not the main problem that the author identifies in relation to euthanasia and thus does not sufficiently answer the question posed. D is irrelevant. E might rectify a problem relating to euthanasia - the cost of keeping people alive, but definitely not the main problem that the author identifies in the extract. B would likely rectify the problem of a seriously ill person not being able to choose - since this analysis is as close to choice as is possible given the extenuating circumstances.

7. B is the correct answer. A is too far removed from the term to suggest that it is the reason she used it. C is the alternative answer most likely to be considered correct, but does not quite fit. The paragraph about how 'it's what they would have wanted' is irrelevant for those who have not yet passed. It would be illogical for the author to start the paragraph with a discussion that people should think further about what they say and then go on to argue something completely different. D cannot be correct as it suggests that the argument that follows is useless, but this is incorrect, the author in fact acknowledges that the statement is clearly true. E is incorrect as it cannot follow simply from using the term 'knee jerk', that the argument that follows is either good or bad, the author goes onto explain this herself in as many words, so cannot expect the term 'knee jerk' to make that implication. B is correct as the adjective 'knee jerk' casts doubt upon the value of the following statement, suggesting that it has not been sufficiently analysed or evaluated.

Extract 3

8. D is the correct answer. A is impossible to know for sure, B is an opinion, C required knowledge of how the poll was expected to go (which is not given in this piece). D is correct as 8/10 (i.e. *most*) of people who admitted to illegally downloading music also said that they bought music.

9. E is the correct answer. A is irrelevant. B, C and D make the evidence questionable. E makes the evidence simply false.

10. B is the correct answer. This is the only statement of opinion: 'need'. The others are clearly all fact. The students might get confused about E. This is still a statement of fact as there is a condition in there - not that they *will* rise, but that they can *expect* to, based on the data.

Extract 4

11. C is the correct answer. C is too draconian. B is incorrect as the schools are obliged to hand over the information. Both D and E are specifically referred to in the piece as not being correct, as Fairport central school district was found to be non-compliant when they only gave over the information once they had received consent. C is the correct interpretation of the law.

12. D is the correct answer. D is the only opinion that is not specifically stated in the extract. Although Tina Weishaus alludes to the idea that the strong tactics used by the recruiters are inappropriate for children, this is not *stated*. Thus, D, if anything, is inferred by the reader from Ms Weishaus' statement.

13. A is the correct answer. C is clearly incorrect. B may at first glance seem correct but the question asks what is the *purpose* of the inclusion of the *phrase*. The use of language may well add something to the piece, but we are not discussing why the author has used that particular literary device. We are discussing the reason the *phrase* is included, and as such it follows that the phrase is included to add something to the argument, namely to draw attention to it.

14. D is the correct answer. All of the answers can be inferred from the figures given. Most students clearly don't want to be approached, as 95% of them didn't consent. Given that recruitment among seniors hit 2% it is fair to assume that most of the 5% who consented must have come from the senior class, thereby suggesting that they are more likely to consent than younger students. Finally, it would be fair to assume that, given that recruitment figures were fairly high among seniors, that the current recruitment strategies work best amongst this group of students.

Extract 5

15. B is the correct answer. The students will probably end up with a choice between A and B. The correct answer is B because in the first paragraph the author clearly states 'our best theories of physics imply we shouldn't be here'. It cannot be said to be 'inexplicable' as clearly, given the piece, there could be an explanation. Thus, A is incorrect. C is incorrect as it is too strong a suggestion - that it 'can' be explained instead of it 'might' be explained. D is simply incorrect as our best theories *do not* explain our existence, and E is too strong a conclusion - it is never stated that no answer will ever be found.

16. C is the correct answer. This is described in the paragraph beginning 'So Vachaspati and his colleagues…'. Only C is identified and all others are clearly incorrect – this should be a fairly simple question as long as the candidates are looking in the right place.

17. A is the correct answer. The section in the final paragraph in the hyphens relates to the definition of the term 'new science', so only the description 'stuff beyond the standard model of particle physics' is the definition and as such the answer must be A. Students might be caught out by the section after the hyphens, but this refers to what is required for CP-violation to provide enough matter in the universe, not to the 'new science' definition.

Extract 6

18. D is the correct answer. B and C are both wrong because the author states that it is impossible to keep addressing the new approach as it arises, the issue must be addressed from the source. E is the conclusion of the first counterargument, but it would be incorrect to say that it is the conclusion of the whole article. A was a point that was made, but again was not the *main* conclusion of the article. The answer is D as the final paragraph concludes that the government must adopt a ground-up approach to tackling extremism.

19. B is the correct answer. A is addressed in the first paragraph of the author's counter argument, C is addressed in the second, D in the penultimate paragraph about over-stretched resources in the security and police departments, and E in the discussion of TPIMS. Although those on the 'fringes' of groups are mentioned as a point of concern, the author does not suggest that the measures will encourage people to move out to the fringes of groups, and as such B must be the correct answer.

20. C is the correct answer. A and B are clearly wrong. E is far too vague and cannot be the reason why the example is used. The choice will come down to C or D. D might seem like it might be correct, however, the question asks why the specific example is used. D would have been correct had the question been, 'Why does the author use an example in this instance'. However, the question asks why he uses that *specific* example, so the answer must have some reference to the example used.

21. A is the correct answer. This is the only statement of fact. B suggests that it is 'plain to see', but this is subjective. C suggests that 'we need…'. This too must be an opinion. D is identified as an opinion by the inclusion of the word 'likely'. E is probably the most obvious opinion as the word 'should' is used.

Extract 7

22. B is the correct answer. A would not be in support of the hypothesis. C and E would all be one stage of extraction further away than B. C shows that murders are premeditated, which gives the murdered the opportunity to contemplate the consequences of their actions. E is not particularly compelling as it only questions free citizens, who might and probably do think very differently to murderers. D would eliminate some evidence in favour of the opposition, but does not put forward any evidence of its own. Thus, B is the only option that gives conclusive results.

23. D is the correct answer. A is explicitly mentioned and thus inference is not required. B is impossible to infer as the likelihood of change is not touched upon. C and E are simply incorrect. It can be inferred from the words which the authors choose to use that they have some level of disdain for those who oppose the death penalty. It almost suggests that they oppose it for the sake of opposing it, and that they will not take kindly (as they must 'come to terms with' it) to new information disproving them.

24. D is the correct answer. A is simply incorrect which in turn means that it cannot be E. B is too vague and does not really address why he uses that specific word. In this question, most students will be choosing between C and D. C is not quite right in that it does not address the word itself - it gives the author's motivation but it does not explain why he chooses to use the word 'admittedly'. The reason he chooses this word is to portray reluctance in showing that his argument may be flawed. D addresses this directly.

25. E is the correct answer. D is irrelevant and not touched upon in the piece at all. A, B and C are all discussed in the article as flaws in the research, but on balance, the main reason that the author suggests the studies have attracted criticism is due to the invalidity of the conclusion as a result of insufficient data. This is shown clearly as the author keeps returning to this point through the piece.

Extract 8

26. C is the correct answer. A reader of the piece could infer from what Saadia Zahidi has said that too much attention is spent on youth unemployment, but it is certainly not an assumption made by the authors, and thus the correct answer cannot be A. B is simply incorrect and not suggested in the piece at all. D could be inferred from the fact that they top the ranking, but is definitely not assumed by the authors. E is an assumption made by Klaus Schwab, but the authors make clear that it is not their opinion and thus not their assumption.

27. B is the correct answer. A is not really a description of the index, but rather an opinion of how useful the index will be for employers. C describes the focus of the index, but not the main purpose of the index itself. D, once again, shows how useful the index may be and not what it actually is. E describes only the part of the index that is discussed in detail throughout the extract, but is not the only information contained within it. B is correct as it accurately describes the whole index, and basically is a paraphrasing of the description given in the second paragraph

28. A is the correct answer. B and D are both explicitly stated, so there is no room for implication. C takes the idea a little too far, and it cannot be said that Schwab intended to imply that people are naive based on what he said. E again is far too extreme to have been implied. A is the correct answer as he suggests that one thing is important and then goes on the state 'we must look beyond campaign cycles and quarterly reports'. This wording implies that he considers that these are not worth spending time on.

Extract 9

29. B is the correct answer. B is the most relevant emotion. Kolby clearly states that the situation is fairly positive at the moment, but has the potential to get worse. B is the only option that takes into account both of these feelings.

30. A is the correct answer. B is mentioned as something that may become a problem in the future, it would not be right to infer from this that chytrid is always supervirulent, in fact it is shown that in some cases (such as this) it is not. C and D are both stated in the article and thus there is no scope for them to have been inferred. E cannot be correct as it would be too far to assume that chytrid is not harmful to any frog – the article shows that in this specific case, for some unknown reason, it is not currently harmful to the frogs in Madagascar. A is the correct answer as the statement 'It could mean we just caught it very early' coupled with the knowledge that the frogs had chytrid on their skin but are not sick would logically lead to an inference that it takes a while for chytrid to make the frogs sick.

31. E is the correct answer. A and C are explicitly mentioned in the final paragraph, whereas the reproduction centres mentioned are not restricted to only Madagascan frogs.

Extract 10

32. D is the correct answer. This is the only answer that conveys sadness, the rest all have an element of disapproval or anger.
33. C is the correct answer. A is incorrect as she clearly goes on to say that these experiences are normal for a child going through a parental separation. B is incorrect as she mentions she had trouble deciding whether to tell her friends about her new familial situation. D is incorrect as she demonises Baynes for making 'gross generalisations'. E is not even touched upon in the piece. C is stated in the paragraph beginning 'I had some really horrible times…'

34. A is the correct answer. This is in reference to where the author states that it is 'gut-wrenching, whatever the circumstances, to watch your dad pack his things into sports bags and leave the family home'. In order to make this statement, she has assumed that there is no possible scenario in which a child would be happy to see their father leave, or else she could not have used the phrase 'whatever the circumstances'. B is incorrect as the author makes no assumptions about how logical resentment is as a response, merely states that it was experienced within her family. C is incorrect as she only refers to Dolce and Gabbana as an example of how Baynes' article made her feel and does not suggest that they believe anything other than what they have said that they think. D is incorrect as she does not compare how she was after the break up to how she was before the break up. She notes how unhappy the new family dynamics made her but does not suggest that she would have been happier had the break up not occurred. E is the opposite of what she suggests in her discussion of Dolce and Gabbana's comments on IVF children.

35. C is the correct answer. The author uses the term 'poison dart' after discussing that Baynes' may well be justified in speaking about her family in a negative way. This suggests that the term relates to only the extension of the argument to include all gay parents. Both B and D must be incorrect, as it has been shown that the author does not dislike the whole of Baynes' argument. A is incorrect as there is no question of what is the most important part of her argument, merely the most damning part.

Extract 11

36. D is the correct answer. All of the answers are potential reasons that the author started the piece in this way
37. B is the correct answer. A is discussed in the first section. C and D are mentioned explicitly in Dr Pardo-Guerra's discussion of AI in the financial sector. E is discussed in relation to Netflix. B is the correct answer as the article discusses how there are certain elements of human behaviour that computers simply cannot predict.
38. A is the correct answer. C is purely incorrect. E is irrelevant. D is true but cannot be said to be the main reason that AI beings are inferior. A and B are both identified in the piece as being restrictions that AI beings have, however, A is discussed first and at further length than B, and so it must be concluded that it is the main reason that the author considers that AI beings are inferior.
39. B is the correct answer. B is the only thing that is actually *implied* by the author in the piece. She notes that 'computers are becoming king', and not just in the tech sector. This is an explicit explanation of A. C is described in her rhetorical question that it may become 'dull' and D is discussed in the final section, with 'And the good news is there is still room for the human touch - at least for now'

Extract 12

40. E is the correct answer. The US position is given in two halves, the first in the very first sentence, and the second at the end of the paragraph. Thus, the answer must be in two parts, so either D or E. E is the correct answer as C is more similar to the wording given in the article, and is marginally different to the meaning in A so both cannot be correct.

41. C is the correct answer. The author uses the phrase 'The FDA and USDA actually had the audacity to include in the draft position…'. The use of the word audacity is the inspiration for this question. Although all of A through to D could be correct the *best* description of the author's position must be C, given that C is a synonym of the word 'audacious' as explicitly mentioned in the piece.

42. A is the correct answer. C is clearly incorrect as it argues against the statement given. D is an 'ad hominem' argument and only undermines the person, not the person's argument. B proves that there is support for the US position but does not disprove the author's position. An article may well undermine the position if backed up by evidence, but that is unknown. The publishing on an article may not address the issues the author raises and as such would not be as damning as the disproval of the studies that that author identifies.

END OF SECTION

Mock Paper B: Section B

1. **Tennessee currently protects teachers who wish to teach children to explore the potential value of following creationism. Do you think that this is correct? Identify and analyse any legal problems that may arise in discussion of this law.**

For - Point

- Freedom of speech should apply to teachers as much as anyone else
- Students should be given the opportunity to choose between evolution and creationism.
- It is possible to teach creationism in a critical and analytical way so as to allow children to decide themselves on what they should believe.
- This in turn will help ensure that science class is about critical discussion rather than just imbibing facts - education instead of indoctrination
- The bill doesn't exclude evolution from being taught alongside creationism - it merely allows room for other theories to be taught.
- Evolution will still be taught in school, but the bill creates more options an opens up academic enquiry

For – Counterpoint

- This is not a simple freedom of speech issue.
- Teachers have freedom of speech in their own time, but during their working hours they have a responsibility to only teach what is relevant to their pupils.
- For example, teachers should not tell their student their own opinions on certain issues, nor should they divulge personal information - their job is to teach fact and curriculum
- Creationism can be taught in a religious context, but should be kept out of schools. Evolution should remain in science classes
- Allowing room for other 'theories' may not be an accurate portrayal of the situation. Impartiality and objectivity is something to strive towards, but creationism is not just another 'theory', it is active denial of scientific fact, and as such should not be fit within an academic environment
- Teaching purely evolution does not mean that students cannot discuss and analyse how well evolution fits with the facts - it can still give rise to a valid discursive environment.
- Furthermore, whilst we want children to be critical of what they are being taught, a large part of education is about the transferral of information and fact - it is widely accepted now that creationism does not have its roots in fact and as such the teaching of it could confuse children.

Against – Point

- Teachers do not and should not have the freedom to teach whatever they want as fact
- Teachers should have to stick to a syllabus
- Children should be given a rounded education that includes knowledge and how to critically analyse that knowledge. However, including too many options in early education could confuse a child. In primary school children should be taught what science is, and then critical analysis could be incorporated at a later date.
- Children should have the right not to be misled by their teachers.
- Telling children that evolution and climate change are scientifically controversial is misleading, as there is no controversy amongst scientists
- Creationism is not science and should not be taught as such
- Science requires testability and falsifiability, which is satisfied by the theory of evolution, and not creationism

Against – Counterpoint

- It is never too early to teach students the value of questioning ideas and theories.
- Just taking the consensus view because it is the consensus view does not encourage students to question what they are told. We do not want students to just believe everything they are told, we want them to be critical and decide for themselves.
- Teaching children only one viewpoint could mislead them into thinking that the issue is fact and settled.
- Arguably, evolution cannot be tested either

2. "There is a time and a place for censorship of the internet." Discuss with particular reference to the right of freedom of expression.

For - Point

- It is the purpose of the government to protect its citizens from harmful sites
- Certain social media sites can be used to harm others, via cyber bullying resulting in psychological and even physical damage. More recently sinister terrorism recruitment sites have become more proactive and successful in recruiting young people. These results can and should be protected against, and the best way to do so is with censorship
- The government has a right to restrict free speech in certain circumstances
- People can express their beliefs and opinions but only where it does not impact other people's human rights. For example we restrict the expression of racial hatred.
- Protection of people from cyber harm would be a logical extension to the valid restrictions on the freedom of speech
- Other forms of media are already regulated
- Newspapers and books are subject to censorship, as are television and film. The internet is arguably more dangerous by virtue of its accessibility, so should be censored in the same way.
- Even sites that everyone thought were innocent have been used in devastating ways
- For example - rioters organising themselves via Facebook and instant messenger. London riots resulted in numerous acts of criminal damage, theft and violence towards others.
- In order to protect people the government must be able to censor sites that can be used disruptively

For – Counterpoint

- Social networking sites can be used malevolently, but they can also be used as a force for good. Surely we should not censor a site which has the potential to do good just because it also has the potential to have a negative impact.
- At what point do we decide that something's negative impact outweighs the potential value of its impact?
- Perhaps censorship *can* be justified but only where the site is objectively and completely harmful and thus the justification of protecting citizens can be used.
- Banning prejudice does not actually address the problem. Perhaps a better way to deal with the issues that arise on the internet, particularly those that arise on social media sites is to engage with it publicly, rather than trying to avoid it.
- The internet is different from other forms of media, in that it is a forum for free information and expression for individuals rather than corporations. Its value is in its freedom and to censor it is to change it irrevocably.
- As a proportion of the number of people who actually use these sites, those who misuse them are very small.
- The site was merely the platform and not the reason behind the disenchantment. The government will be continually chasing these people around the internet from site to site - censoring the site will not address the problem.

Against – Point

- Censorship is incompatible with the notion of free speech.
- It is hypocritical for a government to give people free speech and them ban certain areas of the internet.
- The internet is a free domain and should not be controlled by the government
- The internet is also international, so it is harder to identify which sites would fall under a particular country's laws and regulations
- Censorship may do more harm than good, particularly in terms of losing respect of the government
- For example, people are so dissatisfied with the dictatorial government in China that there has been growing public outrage and disenchantment with the authority of the government

Against – Counterpoint

- No rights are complete, there can always be a reason for restricting a right if it protects people.
- The relevant question is whether the government should restrict freedom of expression, but about how far into a person's autonomy the paternalistic state can venture under a justification of protectionism.
- Arguably however, if the information within a particular site has the capacity to harm people form a certain state, there is a reason and a justification for governmental intervention
- The government can weigh up whether the potential detriment caused by disenfranchisement is worth the benefit of protecting people online.
- For example, people don't like to pay taxes or for taxes to be raised, but the government has the power and the right to collect and raise taxes if they believe it to be for the good of the people.

3. "The UK should codify its Constitution' Discuss.

For - Point

- England will integrate better with Europe if we have a similar legal foundation.
- For protection. A codified Constitution would help prevent tyrannical leaders coming to power.
- For example, the German Constitution allows the German federal government to declare parties unconstitutional and dissolve them.
- A codified, written Constitution provides framework for a successful separation of powers. This is essential for a system of checks and balances.
- We already have a number of written document outlining different sections of our uncodified Constitution. It wouldn't take a lot to codify everything into one manageable document.

For – Counterpoint

- That suggests that we want to stay within Europe. There's a growing national movement of distrust of Europe and to change our constitution to suit Europe would exacerbate the problem.
- The likelihood of that happening is very small - we still have rules and regulations, they just aren't written down in one document.
- Does it though? We wouldn't necessarily be changing the way that our political system works - our executive would still be within our legislature.
- We shouldn't do something just because it might be easy - there needs to be a valid reason for doing it.
- Furthermore it may not be as easy as it seems - there are a number of elements of our constitution that are not enshrined in writing

Against – Point

- Codification of the Constitution eradicates the flexibility of our current uncodified Constitution.
- Sometimes extreme action can be necessary to protect people in new and changing circumstances (e.g. infringing on people's privacy rights in order to protect about new forms of terrorism). Having a codified constitution inhibits quick and efficient action.
- Too much emphasis on the letter of the law leads to an obsession with the text itself and can result in laws that don't quite fit with current popular opinion
- One danger of codifying a constitution is to give the judiciary too much power.
- One of the great things about Britain's common law system is that judges can adapt the law to suit real life situations. Codification could interfere with this and allow unelected officials to 'legislate from the bench'
- Codified constitutions are difficult to change
- A decision to codify our constitution would grant too much power to the government who is able to write it

Against – Counterpoint

- Part of the point of a constitution is to protect people's rights. It is important for a government to have to jump through certain hoops to legitimise their actions. If we don't have sufficient checks and balances the government could be free to abuse their powers.
- Codifying the constitution wouldn't necessarily mean more power for the judiciary. It can be written to protect the system that we already have.
- Furthermore the Constitution can always be changed if it isn't right
- Being resistant to change is the point of a constitution, it provides security.

4. "The general trend towards the liberalisation of marriage undermines its religious basis." Discuss this comment with reference to the idea of abolishing marriage as a legal concept.

For - Point

- Marriage from a religious perspective is between a man and a woman and the liberalisation of this - the rise of divorce and the legalisation of same sex marriage DOES undermine its religious basis, in that it's a union between a man and a woman in the eyes of god.
- This is not, however, necessarily a bad thing - one idea would be to abolish marriage as a legal concept - making a joint union for the purposes of taxation that would be between whoever wants to create that union. Marriage then would be left as a separate union in the eyes of god alone and not in the eyes of the law. Whatever happens to the legal union will be separated from the religious one.
- Religion and the law should be separated, especially given our aim to be a multi-cultural and multi-religious society.
- It is to be unfairly preferential to one group of people to integrate one religion with the law above all others

For – Counterpoint

- Why do we support relationships in the first place - partially mutual support that a long term commitment gives to someone, but also procreation, which is lost by extending it beyond heterosexual couples
- This may be the case if we were creating the law now, but Christianity is inherently connected to the English legal system by virtue of its history and fused past.

Against – Point

- Religious basis is changing - lots of Christians believe that the concept of marriage should be extended to fit in one with modern perceptions

Against – Counterpoint

- But this is only as a response to the law changing what the understanding of marriage is.
- Marriage is traditionally a religious concept and its being integrated with the law means that the religious community has lost control of what marriage is.

END OF PAPER

Mock Paper C: Section A

Extract 1

1. C is the correct answer as the writer mentions in the last paragraph that 'the time will come, and that the present legal conditions of wedlock will be altered in some way or other'. A is wrong because the writer says 'the time has not yet come for any such revolutionary change'. B is wrong as the writer says a change will occur in the future. D is wrong as the writer does not mention the fact that marriage will become 'temporary', this was suggested by Tolstoy in the second last paragraph. E was not mentioned by the writer in the passage.
2. D is the correct answer. Tolstoy mentions that 'the relations between the sexes are searching for a new form', meaning that marriage as a concept is evolving. Whilst A is not entirely wrong, it does not show that marriage is evolving as opposed to being outdated. Tolstoy does not mention B, C or E.
3. A is the correct answer as the writer mentions that 'people are always interested in matrimony' (B), 'marriage has been the hardy perennial of newspaper correspondence' (C), 'whether it be a serious dissertation…or a banal discussion' (D) and 'well-worn' (E). Only A is not mentioned by the writer.
4. A is the correct answer as hardy is not being used as a criticism – rather it is being used to show how marriage has been an 'unfailing resource'. Silly, banal, superficial and distasteful all connote a form of criticism.

Extract 2

5. E is the correct answer as the writer mentions that nature and nurture are 'so widely current'. B is wrong as Shakespeare was the one that created the terms, Galton merely popularised it. C is wrong as the writer is criticising Galton's use of the terms. D is also wrong as the writer says only environmental influences do not undergo much change.
6. D is the correct answer as the writer is referring to humans as a whole. A is wrong as the writer does not mention that 'Man' is the official name of a species, B is wrong as the writer is not trying to emphasise the importance, and E is wrong as it is the opposite of what the writer is trying to refer to.
7. B is the correct answer as the writer mentions that 'nature vs. nurture cannot be solved in general terms' and 'can be understood only be examining one trait at a time'. A is wrong as it is the opposite of B, and C, D and E do not reflect precisely what the author said in the passage.
8. C is the correct answer. Soil and climate are not being used as a contrasting pair, rather they are being referred to as related examples. The rest of the pairs are all used as contrasting pairs by the writer.

Extract 3

9. E is the correct answer as the writer states that biology 'is a generic term applied to a large group of biological sciences all of which alike are concerned with the phenomena of life'. A-D are not mentioned by the writer.
10. C is the correct answer. C was presented as a fact by the writer in the second paragraph, whereas A, B, D and E were all opinions of the writer and the writer did not claim that these were facts.
11. C is the correct answer as the writer states in the second paragraph that the biologist 'may not hope to solve the ultimate problems of life…'. A, B, D and E were all mentioned by the writer as issues that a biologist may resolve.
12. A is the correct answer as A is the only option that does not refer to the metaphor of a 'machine', whereas B-E all refer or relate to the 'machine' metaphor.

Extract 4

13. B is the correct answer as B is given only as an example by the writer, whereas A, C, D and E all introduce a new argument.
14. A is the correct answer as only A was used as a complete definition of fossils by the writer, B-D were not exhaustive definitions of fossils and E is also wrong as a result.
15. A is the correct answer as 'animals' and 'plants' were referred to as a collective, not as a direct comparison, whereas B-E were all used as direct comparisons.
16. B is the correct answer as the writer explains in the last paragraph that 'unless the conditions were such as to preserve at least the hard parts of any creature from immediate decay, there was small probability of it becoming fossilised'. A, C and D were not mentioned by the writer, and hence E is wrong as well.

Extract 5

17. A is the correct answer as the writer alludes to this in the first paragraph by stating that 'Sanskrit was the eldest sister of them all'. Hence all the other options are wrong.
18. C is the correct answer as 'human mind' is being used literally in this passage, whereas the other options are being used metaphorically.
19. B is the correct answer as the writer alludes to this by stating that 'as Sanskrit stepped into the midst of these languages, there came light and warmth and mutual recognition'. A, C and D were not mentioned by the writer, and hence E is wrong as well.
20. C is the correct answer as the writer alludes to this by stating that 'take the words which occur in the same form and with the same meaning…'. A, B and D were mentioned by the writer but were not suggested as precise ways of understanding a language but merely examples, and hence E is wrong as well.

Extract 6

21. E is the correct answer. The writer suggests this by stating that 'we must teach nature…but we must not, in so doing, wean still more from, but perpetually incite to visit, field, forest, hill…'. A-D do not precisely describe the writer's argument put forward in the last paragraph.
22. A is the correct answer as the writer states in the first paragraph that 8-12 is where the acute stage of teething is passing, not when it is starting. B-E were all mentioned by the writer as happening from 8-12.
23. The correct answer is A as Rosseau states that we should 'leave prepubescent years to nature', and this is agreed on by the writer in the last paragraph. B-D are wrong as Rosseau argues that children should grow up in the wild independently, whereas the writer argues that we should be supplementing reading with outdoor activity. Hence E is wrong as well.
24. E is the correct answer as E provides the best summary of the author's argument in the last paragraph, whereas A-D do not reflect the writer's argument.

Extract 7

25. C is the correct answer as the writer mentions that 'we must still be permitted to doubt if the time has even yet arrived…can be appreciated in accordance with his just value'. This suggests that the writer thinks Chopin's work may be underrated, and hence the other options are wrong.
26. B is the correct answer as this was alluded to by the writer in the second paragraph where he states 'is it not equally true that…are never recognised as prophets in their own times?'. Hence, the other options are wrong.
27. D is the correct answer, as 'composition' is being used in a more literal sense as compared to the other options.
28. C is the correct answer as the writer alludes to this when he says that 'musicians who do not restrict themselves within the limits of conventional routine…more need than other artists of the aid of time'. The other options are a misreading of the writer's argument.

Extract 8

29. C is the correct answer as the writer comes off as being critical about the argument that morality and religion are related. The other options do not fit the tone the writer has adopted.
30. E is the correct answer as all the philosophers mentioned agree about the lack of connection between morality and religion.
31. A is the correct answer as only A argues that morality and religion are related, whereas the other options disagree.
32. A is the correct answer as 'backward' is not used negatively in the first paragraph, it simply refers to the past, whereas the other options are used negatively.

Extract 9

33. E is the correct answer as the writer states this in the last paragraph by saying 'Australia was the last part of the world to be thus visited and explored'. Hence the other options are wrong.
34. C is the correct answer as this was stated in the last paragraph when the writer mentioned 'scarcely any one cared to run the risk of exploring it'. The other options were not cited as reasons for not exploring Australia.
35. D is the correct answer as this was cited in the first paragraph where the writer states that 'they believed the man who could penetrate far enough would find countries where inexhaustible riches were to be gathered'. The other options were not cited as reasons for venturing into the unknown.
36. A Is the correct answer as only A was not mentioned as a factor behind the ability to travel in the passage. A was cited as a motivation instead.

Extract 10

37. D is the correct answer, as the writer alludes to this in the last paragraph by saying that 'but the explanation of the phenomenon and the name that is given to it matters little…it constitutes…the principal material of which we shape our dreams'. The rest were mentioned by the author as periphery matters instead of the heart of the question.
38. E is the correct answer as the writer merely states some examples of opinions in the last paragraph, but does not show that there is a consensus. A-D were all cited as examples of differences in opinions.
39. A is the correct answer, as the writer only agrees with the fact that we see colours when we close our eyes, but does not attempt to agree on what are mentioned in B-D. Hence E is wrong as well.

Extract 11

40. C is the correct answer, as this was stated in the last paragraph when the writer mentioned that 'pathological lying is very rarely the single offense of the pathological liar'. The other options were not mentioned by the writer.
41. D is the correct answer as this was mentioned in the third paragraph when the writer states that 'where the individual by the virtue of language ability endeavours to maintain a place in the world which his abilities do not otherwise justify'. The other options are a misreading of what the write explains using Case 12.
42. C is the correct answer, as the writer is providing an academic analysis of the condition of pathological liars, as opposed to adopting a different tone suggested by the other options.

END OF SECTION

Mock Paper C: Section B

1. Is social media damaging for teenagers?

Argument (For)

- Social media is damaging to teenagers because it lowers their self-esteem.
- Social media is flooded with pictures of good-looking people and unrealistic body images that perpetuates a need for teenagers to pursue that image.
- Excessive consumption of social media has been linked to lower self-confidence and a higher rate of depression amongst teenagers, especially amongst girls who are more likely to be affected by a lack of confidence in their body and looks.

Counter-point

- Social media does not always necessarily lead to lower self-esteem and perpetuate an unhealthy body image.
- Social media can be used to share uplifting posts, encouraging messages, and it is also a good platform to spread awareness of certain issues.
- Social media is a double-edged sword and can be used for good or bad, and if utilised correctly it can be useful in increasing the awareness of important issues such as fighting against eating disorders and mental disorders.

Argument (Against)

- Social media does more good than harm to teenagers as it allows teenagers to express themselves more and provides an outlet for them to showcase their creativity.
- For example, some teenagers may showcase their photography skills through Instagram, or video-editing and producing skills through YouTube, and they can receive support easily from their peers through such social media website.

Counter-point

- Even though such social media platforms provide an opportunity for teenagers to showcase their creativity, they are more often than not used to showcase frivolous material and perpetuate low-level humour.
- For example, YouTube is flooded with distasteful videos and the latest drama involving Logan Paul shows how the content available in YouTube usually leaves much to be desired.

Argument (For)

- Social media is damaging to teenagers as it leads to an obsession with popularity and creates an unhealthy culture of emphasising the need for validation.
- Teenagers are increasingly obsessed with having more followers on Instagram and having more likes for their pictures, and this creates a situation where many young girls are posting revealing pictures in order to garner more followers and likes, when they are too young to understand the consequences and repercussions of doing so.

Counter-point

- Not all teenagers see social media as a platform for increasing their popularity and receiving validation from strangers.
- Many teenagers use social media as an efficient platform for connecting with and keeping in touch with their friends and families, especially when they are geographically separated.
- Social media platforms such as Facebook provide a good method for teenagers to easily stay in touch with their friends and families and be updated about their lives.

Argument (Against)

- Social media is potentially very dangerous for teenagers due to a rise in the number of sexual predators utilising social media to take advantage of teenagers.
- There have been many reported cases of sexual predators posing as someone on Facebook in order to establish contact with a teenager, and later on coerce them into doing sexual acts or sexually grooming them.
- The lack of adequate safeguards and parental control over a teenager's use of social media makes it potentially very dangerous.

Counter-point

- The use of social media platforms will not be dangerous as long as adequate safeguards are put in place.
- For example, parental control can be implemented on social media sites, and social media companies are taking down false accounts or suspicious activities and posts in order to reduce incidents of sexual predators searching for victims on social media sites.

2. To what extent should journalists be responsible for 'fake news'?

Argument (For)

- Journalists have a huge influence on the public and should be responsible for ensuring that whatever they publish is accurate and not misleading.
- It has been argued that misleading news have led to more people voting in favour of Brexit than there would be had certain news outlets been more responsible in portraying accurate facts that were not sensationalist and misleading.
- Journalists should be held responsible should they fail to fulfil their duties and lead to the public being misinformed.

Counter-point

- Journalists are merely responsible for conveying facts and opinions, it is up to the public to be discerning in reading the news and forming an opinion themselves.
- Different news outlets are allowed to have different political opinions – for example, The Guardian is known to be left-wing in general whilst The Daily Mail tends to be more right-wing.
- Journalists should not be held responsible if someone fails to read critically and takes what the newspapers say as the gospel.

Argument (Against)

- Making journalists responsible for 'fake news' will be a serious impediment to the freedom of speech and the need for news outlets to be independent and allowed to voice their opinions and independent thoughts.
- Trump's allegations that journalists are irresponsible and often write 'fake news' in order to incite hate fails to take into account the fact that freedom of speech is a fundamental right behind journalism and without such freedom the public will not be able to learn about both sides of the argument.

Counter-point

- As important as freedom of speech is, such freedom should be exercised responsibly and journalists should be held responsible if they fail to verify facts and only focus on increasing readership by posting sensationalist and controversial news.
- The general public may not always be very discerning or have the time or initiative to read widely from different sources, and they may easily believe the first thing they read and be affected as a result.
- Hence, journalists have an inherent duty to ensure that what they are reporting are factually accurate as much as possible.

Argument (For)

- Fake news is potentially highly dangerous to society as journalists are capable of inciting hate in the public and this may lead to a division amongst different religious and racial groups, which leads to social disintegration.
- Journalists need to exercise a level of responsibility in ensuring that they are not publishing news that denounce a certain racial or religious group, and ensure that they take into account the sensitivity and delicacy of the situation before posting any news article that might incite hate.

Counter-point

- The journalists job is simply to report on facts and opinions and they should not be treated as politicians and be a moral arbiter in deciding what news should be published and what should not be in the interest of the public.
- It is important for journalists to publish any news or facts that the public deserves to know instead of being limited by cultural sensitivities or controversial topics, as without such publications the public will be deceived about what is going on and will not be properly informed about current affairs.

Argument (Against)

- It is not appropriate to make journalists liable for 'fake news' as it is ultimately the readers fault for not verifying the source of the article or cross-referring to other publications.
- Journalists are not public figures and they are not expected to be held to a standard and scrutinised the same way that we would do with elected politicians or academics with an established standing.
- The job scope of a journalist does not entail making them responsible for 'fake news' – rather, it is up to the public to be discerning about what they read and choose to believe.

Counter-point

- Due to the important nature of news and the increasing importance of journalists in shaping public opinion especially during revolutionary political occasions, they should likewise be held to a high standard and be scrutinised if they fail to fulfil their duties and let down the public as a result.
- We should be elevating the role of a journalist and ensure that they are equally held accountable for misleading the public as would a politician be.

3. Limitations should be put in place for scientific discovery. Discuss.

Argument (For)

- Certain limitations should be placed on scientific discovery due to the potential ethical and moral issues that may arise if scientific discovery was unlimited.
- For example, human cloning poses thorny ethical issues and despite the perceived benefits such discovery may bring to mankind, it carries potentially unethical outcomes such as flouting human rights and creating an unprecedented morality issue.
- Genetic engineering is another area where even though the potential benefits are great, but it may lead to unethical outcomes such as 'designer babies' or only allowing the rich to alter their genes beneficially.

Counter-point

- Scientific discovery is limitless and if limitations are sought against scientific discovery, mankind will not be able to progress quickly and we will not be able to resolve many problems plaguing society nowadays.
- For example, research on GMO food can potentially resolve nutritional deficiencies in developing countries, but due to religious backlash, such research has not received adequate funding and regulatory approval.
- Genetic engineering is also an area that can possibly lead to cures for certain genetic diseases such as Parkinson's disease, but limitations put in place will severely slow down any progress that can be made.

Argument (Against)

- We should not place limitations on scientific discovery as there can never be a consensus on certain ethical, morality and religious issues, and the progress of society and technology should not be impeded by the opposite of certain religious or fundamentalist groups.
- For example, stem cell research has proven to contain immense potential in helping to find cures for genetic diseases, yet certain religious groups are against such research as they deem an embryo to be a human life and thus extracting stem cells from an embryo is deemed against their religious values.
- Such limitations are damaging and can slow down the discovery of important solutions to debilitating diseases that plague many individuals.

Counter-point

- Even though the need to find a cure for genetic diseases is pressing, we cannot ignore morality or ethical issues that can arise from such research.
- Certain controversial research such as stem cell research, if left unlimited, may lead to a slippery slope where scientists are not afraid to do anything in the name of advancing science.
- This can lead to extreme situations where human testing is allowable in the name of progressing science.
- Not all methods of advancing science are ethical, and we need to draw a line between what is permissible and what is not.

Argument (For)

- Limitations on scientific research is needed because there are absolute moral rights that should not be infringed and science cannot be used as a reason for flouting such rights.
- For example, torturing a human or killing a human for the sake of scientific discovery will never be permissible, even if it is in the name of medical discovery, as the right to live is an absolute human right that should never be infringed.
- In less clear cut areas, such as stem cell research or genetic engineering, the pros and cons need to be weighed carefully in deciding whether certain research should be allowed in order to improve technologies, and scientists need to always ensure that they have adequately considered the ethical issues arising before conducting research.

Counter-point

- Scientific discovery can be used to save and improve millions of lives and if limitations are put in place to hinder such discovery, we are essentially allowing millions of people to die from a lack of cure to their sickness or exposure to dangerous elements.
- Scientific discovery needs to advance quickly in order to provide a solution to numerous fatal diseases that have no cure as of now due to the limited nature of scientific discovery, and mankind will benefit as a whole with scientific discovery being made unlimited.

Argument (Against)

- Scientific research is inherently expensive, and scientists need to be incentivised in order to produce quality research and unravel the complexities of science.
- Instead of placing further limits and hindering scientific research further, we should be doing more to catalyse scientific research instead, such as having more funding opportunities and initiatives for scientists to engage in their research.
- More people should also be willing to sacrifice in the name of benefiting science and discovery, such as opting to donate their organs when they die so that such organs can either be used to save another life or be used for important scientific research.

Counter-point

- Not all scientists may be engaging in research and development for altruistic purposes, and some may harbour bad intentions or may be purely looking at making a profit.
- If we leave scientific discovery unlimited, this creates a huge risk of scientists abusing their powers and benefiting from their research more than what the public stands to gain as a result.
- They may create a cure for HIV, but acquire rights over the cure and sell the drug at such a high price in order to make a profit that only the rich can afford such a cure.
- Hence, limits need to be put in place in order to ensure that scientific discovery will benefit mankind.

4. **Too many students are going to University. Discuss.**

Argument (For)

- Too many students are going to universities, and many of these students end up unemployed, or being over-qualified for jobs that place a greater emphasis on skills and know-how.
- Having too many university graduates causes a mismatch between the demand and supply of jobs, and students become increasingly disenfranchised after spending many years in university and paying a substantial amount of tuition fees, only to find out that they cannot get the jobs that they want.
- Many degrees are also irrelevant to the job market, and students end up being ill-suited for the kind of jobs that require employees.

Counter-point

- Going to university is more than just preparing students for work.
- University also provides a good opportunity for students to mature and develop, and acquire an important network of friends.
- Furthermore, university not only teaches academic content but also teaches crucial soft skills that are highly demanded in the workforce such as teamwork, leadership skills, communication skills, writing skills and negotiating skills.
- University provides a good opportunity in terms of training a student's mind and a more highly-educated populace is desirable because it allows the populace to be more discerning and well-informed.

Argument (Against)

- University education is important as it provides a good opportunity for students to discover what they enjoy doing and what they are good at, and gives them a safe ground for developing their potential and capabilities.
- Even though not all students go on to work in a field that is relevant to their degree, university education is important nonetheless as it trains students to think critically and be able to evaluate information and convey it in a clear manner – something that is highly emphasised on in the workforce.

Counter-point

- University education is becoming increasingly unaffordable and despite the perceived benefits of university education, too many students do not take university seriously and end up wasting their time in university and racking up a huge amount of debt as a result without any tangible benefits upon graduating.
- This problem is particularly acute in lower-ranked universities that have less stringent academic requirements and rigour, which results in many students not learning much during their university education and incurring unnecessary debt.

Argument (For)

- It has come to a point where universities are producing degrees en masse and there is too much emphasis on quantity over quality.
- Too many degrees being handed out results in the value of a degree being depressed as a result, and no one will take a degree seriously if everyone has a degree.
- Universities are exploiting the demand for degrees by having lax standards and low entry requirements, which results in students who are not academically-inclined being able to enrol into a university and get a degree that is not of much use in the workforce.
- There should be a greater emphasis on quality over quantity and there should be greater focus on ensuring that the education being given is of a high standard, as opposed to being mass-produced.

Counter-point

- Everyone has a basic right to education, and university education should not be limited to the 'elites'.
- The problem with reserving university education only for the top few students is that this results in greater inequality, where poorer students may fail to get an opportunity to have a university education just because they could not afford better teaching or resources in order to do well for their exams.
- Education is the great leveller of society and we should not deprive students of education by making university education reserved only for the elites, hence university education should be more accessible.

Argument (Against)

- University places should not be restricted to the top few universities as even though some universities may not be as highly-regarded or well-ranked as others, they may be able to provide good education in terms of achieving high student satisfaction and providing greater attention between teachers and students.
- University education should be made available for students who have a curiosity to learn and improve themselves, and we should not deprive such students of university education just because they are not as academically-inclined as the 'elite' students'.

Counter-point

- Society should place less emphasis on the need for a degree in order to survive in society.
- There are many countries with far fewer university graduates but high employment rates, such as Germany where many students opt to go into apprenticeships instead in order to acquire skills that cannot be taught in universities.
- We should not place so much emphasis on ensuring that everyone gets to go university, as not everyone is cut out for academic and there are many people that are talented in other areas.
- Alternative education and training should be given more emphasis in order to diversify our talent pool and ensure that students are getting the skills required for jobs and not just going to university for the sake of it.

END OF PAPER

Mock Paper D: Section A

Extract 1

1. D is the correct answer as the writer mentions throughout the passage that the laws only benefited certain classes at the expense of the public. A-C were not mentioned in the passage; hence E is wrong as well.
2. C is the correct answer as this was alluded to in the sentence 'to render the articles which such classes deal in or produce dearer than they would otherwise be if the public was left at liberty to supply itself with such commodities'. The other options are not alluded to in the first paragraph.
3. A is the correct answer as the writer states that patents were initially meant to result in 'exclusive exercise of certain trades or occupations in particular places'. The other options were mentioned as the unintended side-effects of patents.
4. E is the correct answer as the writer does not agree with any of the 'excuses' put forward on behalf of imposition of high duties.

Extract 2

5. A is the correct answer as the writer mentioned at the start of the passage that camouflage is used in 'modern warfare' which refers to humans, as opposed to animals. The other options all refer to animals.
6. E is the correct answer as all the options were mentioned by the writer to describe the two different forms of camouflage developed in nature.
7. E is the correct answer as all the animals mentioned adopt a similar method of camouflage – blending in with their surroundings.
8. C is the correct answer as the writer is providing an analytical review of camouflage in this passage, as opposed to the other tones mentioned.

Extract 3

9. C is the correct answer as the writer capitalises the word 'Nature' as he is referring to it as a distinct entity, as opposed to what the options suggest.
10. A is the correct answer as 'Universe' is used in the literal sense in this passage, whereas the other options are all used metaphorically.
11. A is the correct answer as it is presented as a fact in the first paragraph, whereas the other options are all presented as opinions.
12. B is the correct answer as the writer alludes to this in the last paragraph by mentioning that 'our widest and safest generalisations are simply statements of the highest degree of probability'. The other options were not alluded to in the passage.

Extract 4

13. C is the correct answer as the writer mentions in the second paragraph that selection for breeding differs between artificial selection and natural selection.
14. E is the correct answer as all of the examples were mentioned for examples of 'struggle for existence' behind the natural selection theory.
15. C is the correct answer as only 'avoiding accidents' was not mentioned by the author as a factor behind the selection of the best for reproduction.
16. A is the correct answer as only A was used as an example of artificial selection, not natural selection.

Extract 5

17. D is the correct answer as 'dropping out of one joint' was stated as the main effect of brachydactyly, whereas the other effects mentioned were all side-effects.
18. A is the correct answer as the writer explains in the first paragraph that one affected parent is enough to produce an offspring with brachydactyly, hence only two normal parents will not produce an offspring with the condition.
19. D is the correct answer as the writer explains in the third paragraph that 'in each individual there is a different set of modifying factors or else a variation in the factor'. The other reasons were not stated by the writer as a reason for the difference in seriousness.
20. B is the correct answer as the writer alludes to this in the last paragraph by concluding that 'it must be recognised that every visible character of an individual is the result of numerous factors'. The other options were all listed as examples to support his argument or are wrong.

Extract 6

21. A is the correct answer as the writer states it originated from Gautama of India in the first paragraph.
22. A is the correct answer as the writer states in the first paragraph that 'no further steps' were taken after the emperor set up the image of the Buddha, whereas the other options all contributed to the rise of Buddhism.
23. D is the correct answer as the other options were not given as reasons for the decline of Confucianism.
24. D is the correct answer as this was explained by the writer in the third paragraph where he says that 'this dream story is worth repeating because it goes to show that Buddhism was not only known at an early date…'.

Extract 7

25. C is the correct answer as only C is being used as a matter of fact, the other options are all presented as the writer's opinion.
26. C is the correct answer as this passage is being addressed to universities in general to encourage them to make students study more sciences.
27. C is the correct answer as the writer argues throughout the passage that the sciences are being neglected by students.
28. B is the correct answer as the writer is critical about the lack of education in science in England.

Extract 8

29. C is the correct answer as only C is presented as a fact, whereas the other options were all presented as opinions.
30. E is the correct answer as all the options are being used with a negative connotation in the passage.
31. D is the correct answer as the writer comes across as highly opinionated in the passage as opposed to the other options suggested.
32. C is the correct answer as the writer alludes to this in the last paragraph by stating that 'women's steady march onward, and her growing desire for a broader outlook, prove that she has not reached her normal condition'.

Extract 9

33. E is the correct answer as all the examples mentioned were not the writer's own opinion, rather they were viewpoints of other people.
34. D is the correct answer as the writer states in the second paragraph that analysing Muhammedanism helps us to be able to critically evaluate Christianity.
35. C is the correct answer as only C would be a neutral party who is merely analysing the religions to understand them better as opposed to strengthening their conviction in a particular religion.
36. D Is the correct answer as the writer mentions in the second paragraph that 'the evolution of such a system of belief is best understood by examining a religion to which we have not been bound'.

Extract 10

37. C is the correct answer as the writer is claiming the opposite of C as the reason why he chose yeast as a topic.
38. A is the correct answer as 'succulent' is not being used to describe the formation of yeast, but rather the fruits that are used to form yeast.
39. A is the correct answer as facts and phenomena are being used as a collective and not as a form of comparison.

Extract 11

40. D is the correct answer as both A and B are being illustrated by the examples used by the writer.
41. E is the correct answer as all the examples given are raised as differences between love in mankind and the animal kingdom.
42. B is the correct answer as the writer explains in the last paragraph that there is a scientific reason why good-looking people tend to be favoured.

END OF SECTION

Mock Paper D: Section B

1. Should the voting age be reduced?

Argument (For)

- The voting age should be reduced because policies that are being decided on now will affect young people the most in the future.
- If young people do not get the chance to vote, they do not have a say regarding who should be elected and what policies will be implemented as a result.

Counter-point

- The voting age should not be reduced as young people are not always sufficiently politically-aware in order to make an informed decision and the fact that voter turnout is usually low amongst the youngest age group shows that it is unnecessary for the voting age to be reduced as young people do not know how to exercise their voting rights responsibly.

Argument (Against)

- The voting age should not be reduced as young people are easily influenced and swayed by external opinion and tend to favour populist policies that may well harm their long-term interests.
- For example, young people may be overly-myopic and only focus on issues that provide a tangible benefit to them in the short term, such as lower tuition fees, without considering issues that might affect them in the long run.

Counter-point

- The voting age should be reduced as there is a greater emphasis on political education at a young age these days and many policies being proposed by the political parties have a direct and actual impact on the younger generation.
- Young people are well-equipped and well-informed to exercise their votes responsibly, and should have a say regarding which policies will benefit them the most.

Argument (For)

- The voting age should be reduced as it is unfair that the older generation gets to vote on certain policies that will benefit them at the expense of the younger generation, even though the younger generation will be the ones who have to suffer the consequences of such policies in the long term.
- For example, the older generation may prefer policies such as increasing pension funds, which will mean higher taxes on the younger generation, or bringing back compulsory national service, which will only be applicable for the younger generation.

Counter-point

- The voting age should not be reduced as every generation faces the same problem of not getting a say in the policies being implemented until they are of sufficient age and maturity to make an informed-decision.
- The older generation also once did not get the chance to vote on policies to benefit them, and they are fully-qualified to vote on policies that they think are beneficial for the country with their life experiences and maturity.
- Many older generations will also have children and it is not always true that they will vote on policies that will benefit them at the expense of the younger generation.

Argument (Against)

- The voting age should not be reduced as young people simply lack the maturity and political thoughtfulness to be able to decide which political party will serve the nation's interests.
- Surveys overwhelmingly suggest that young people are ignorant when it comes to politics and have an overly-simplified or non-existent knowledge of current affairs and the nuances in views between different political parties.
- They are too easily swayed by sensationalist and populist arguments made by politicians and they tend to vote without putting in much thought and analysis.

Counter-point

- The voting age should be reduced as young people get increasingly-educated nowadays and many young people are engaging in active discussion about politics online and are discerning when it comes to analysis political news from multiple sources and forming an independent opinion based on the information available.
- The fact that the political inclinations of young people tend to show a marked difference with the older generation simply shows that times have changed and the priorities of young people going forward are vastly different from the older generation.

2. Should tuition fees be reduced?

Argument (For)

- Tuition fees should be reduced as high tuition fees are hindering low-income students from considering higher education, resulting in a lack of social mobility and a denial of the right to education based on income-levels.
- Tuition fees have become increasingly unaffordable in recent years, and this has become a huge deterrent for students who are not from well-to-do families from pursuing higher education, even though they may be academically-capable of doing so.

Counter-point

- Tuition fees should not be reduced as tuition fees are needed for universities to remain competitive and hire the best professors and have the best resources for students in order to ensure quality teaching.
- If tuition fees were reduced, even if more students will be enticed to enrol in university as a result, it will mean that all students will end up receiving sub-standard education with the lack of resources and financial-backing needed.

Argument (Against)

- Tuition fees should not be reduced as there is already the student loan scheme in place which ensures that students only need to start re-paying their loan upon graduation if they earn a certain amount of income.
- This helps to ensure that low-income students will still have easy access to universities, and they will only need to pay off the loans if they manage to secure a job that pays enough for them to repay the loan.

Counter-point

- Tuition fees should be reduced as the high level of tuition fees being charged causes many students to be heavily-indebted upon graduation, causing an immense financial burden to them and provides a disincentive for many students to consider university in the first place, even if they qualified for university academically.

Argument (For)

- Tuition fees should be reduced as universities already have the benefit of huge donations and grants being given by alumni and research organisations in order for them to survive and provide quality education, it is unfair to charge students exorbitant tuition fees and create a high barrier to entry based on financial means.
- The argument that tuition fees are needed to sustain a university is weak in this day and age when the bulk of a university's revenue comes from research grants and legacy donations.

Counter-point

- Tuition fees should not be reduced as not all universities have the benefit of large grants and legacy donations.
- Only the top-ranked universities and the most prestigious universities will be able to attract sufficient funding and donations from successful alumni and be able to survive even without charging high rates of universities.
- Many other universities will struggle to survive without charging sufficiently high tuition fees, and reducing tuition fees might be counter-intuitive and result in less university places being available.

Argument (Against)

- Tuition fees should not be reduced as too many students are going to university for the sake of it and do not take their degree seriously.
- It is well-known that many students in less rigorous courses and universities only treat university as an extra 3-4 years of socialising and partying.
- Taxpayers should not have to subsidise these students when they are not doing something of value and tuition fees should remain as it is in order to act as a deterrent for students who are not naturally inclined for university education in the first place.

Counter-point

- Tuition fees should be reduced as university not only provides academic teaching, it also provides important soft-skills and allows students to figure out what they are good at and what they want to do in life.
- Studies have shown that university education is highly beneficial in terms of a person's success later on in life as well as their earning capacity.
- Hence, we should not deny this opportunity to many students who might otherwise be put off by the high tuition fees.

3. Tourism does more harm than good. Discuss.

Argument (For)

- Tourism does more harm than good as it leads to issues such as gentrification of towns that are heavily visited by tourists.
- Popular destinations such as Paris and Bali have experienced this phenomenon whereby due to the heavy inflow of tourists every year, more and more shops are opened for the benefit of tourists, placing increasing competition on local shops and causing them to close down.
- This leads to an erosion of culture and to a process of gentrification whereby towns with significant culture start to become more standardised with similar shops to cater to the taste of tourists.

Counter-point

- Tourism provides more benefit than harm as tourism is a significant contributor to economic growth in many countries, and has led to the creation of many jobs.
- For example, destinations such as Hawaii are heavily-dependent on tourism for economic growth, and tourists provide a lot of potential economic benefits for the locals, such as sustaining certain trades that might die off without the demand from tourists, as well as sustaining the hospitality industry that is highly lucrative for the home country.

Argument (Against)

- Tourism provides more benefit than harm as tourism allows a greater awareness of the cultural differences between countries and acts as a form of diplomacy between different countries by increasing the level of interaction between people of different nationality.
- Gap years are an example of students being able to experience the culture of different countries if done responsibly and tourism helps open up certain countries to the rest of the world and allow people from all over the world to appreciate the beauty of a country.

Counter-point

- Tourism is more harmful than good as many tourists do not visit a country with an open-mind and there are many instances of tourists being an annoyance to their host country and causing discontent amongst the locals.
- For example, there are stories of tourists vandalising cultural artefacts in the host country, or tourists disrespecting the local culture of a country by dressing inappropriately or taking inappropriate photos. Students on gap years also often do so irresponsibly by partaking in activities that exploit the host country and are unethical without realising it.

Argument (For)

- Tourism causes more harm than good as it leads to environmental degradation, erosion of cultural sites and also contributes to a larger carbon footprint.
- Many tourists visit cultural sites without being responsible and helping to conserve such sites, and a high human traffic often leads to an acceleration of the degradation of heritage sites and an erosion of the natural beauty of a cultural site.
- Tourism also encourages a large amount of travelling by airplanes and trains which contribute significantly to the rising global carbon footprint.

Counter-point

- Tourism does more good than harm as tourism is becoming increasingly more sophisticated these days and many cultural and heritage sites are protected in order to preserve them, allowing tourists to fully enjoy the beauty of such places without destroying them.

- For example, there are plenty of UNESCO heritage sites that are being actively protected and works are often done in order to restore such sites and maintain them. Technology has also increasingly allowed more environmentally-friendly travel options to be made available, such as electric cars and bullet trains.

Argument (Against)

- Tourism is more beneficial than harmful as it closes the distance between countries and allows more individuals to be exposed to different cultures and practices that they would not be able to experience back at home.
- This fosters a more liberal and understanding mindset and well-travelled individuals will tend to be more well-informed, culturally-aware and accepting of differences due to their interactions.
- If tourism was reduced, more people would be insular and fail to understand differences between cultures due to their limited exposure and interactions with different people.

Counter-point

- Tourism causes more harm than good as it provides an artificial image of a country to tourists and merely scratches the surface, without allowing tourists to fully understand the way of living and the difficulties faced by a country.
- For example, a tourist will not be expected to have fully-immersed in the local culture if they spend a week in a luxury resort, without any interactions with the locals, and only visit tourist attractions that are catered and commercialised for tourists.
- This leads to great misconceptions about countries and does not allow a greater cultural awareness.

4. Banning the wearing of a headscarf in the public sector is discriminatory. Discuss.

Argument (For)

- Banning the wearing of a headscarf in the public sector is discriminatory as this causes a natural barrier for religious Muslim women who wish to enter the public sector, but are not allowed to exercise their freedom of expression of religion accordingly.
- This ban hence deters Muslim women from applying for public sector jobs especially if their religion is a fundamental part of their identity and they strongly believe in the requirement to wear a headscarf in public.

Counter-point

- Banning the wearing of a headscarf in the public sector is not discriminatory if it is done for a legitimate reason, and the ban extends to other forms of religious expression as well.
- For example, a legitimate reason will be that the public sector has to appear as secular and must not be affiliated with any religious belief.
- Hence, if headscarves are banned because of their affiliation with Islam, along with other forms of religious clothing such as wearing a cross for Christians or wearing a turban for Sikhs, such a ban will be justified.

Argument (Against)

- Such a ban is not discriminatory as it is within the control of applicants to decide whether or not they are suitable for a job and are able to adhere to the dress code.
- Many jobs require specific dress codes, such as the military and uniformed services, and we should not relax our standards just to cater to one particular group especially if there is a strong reason for the dress code, such as uniformity and symbolism.
- Hence, as long as the ban is not specifically directed towards a particular religion, but rather a general requirement of specific clothing that should be worn, it is not discriminatory.

Counter-point

- Such a ban is discriminatory as even though the ban is not a direct ban on Muslim women from serving in the public sector, they are indirectly discriminated against and suffer a disproportionate effect as they as a collective group are more likely to be required to wear a headscarf as per their religious norms.
- Having such a ban will result in much fewer Muslim women being able to apply for the job as it will go against their religious convictions, and this constitutes indirect discrimination against them.

Argument (For)

- Such a ban is discriminatory as there is no legitimate reason why the wearing of a headscarf will interfere with the job of working in the public sector.
- If wearing a headscarf will not interfere with the ability of the worker to complete her job, such a ban will not be justified and will be discriminatory.
- This is in contrast to jobs where eye-contact may be important, such as a teaching job for example, where in that case a burka might be unsuitable as it reduces the amount of eye contact between the teacher and student and interferes with the student's learning abilities.

Counter-point

- Such a ban is not discriminatory as there is an expectation in the public sector that the workers are representing the state, and there is a legitimate reason for expecting that a headscarf should not be worn, especially if it might cause discomfort amongst certain members of the public or if it will give rise to the wrong idea about the public sector.
- These are precautionary measures that have to be taken for a sensitive sector such as the public sector and candidates should be aware of these additional requirements before applying for such jobs.

Argument (Against)

- The ban is not discriminatory as such a ban can be justified if it is restricted to the more public-facing and sensitive roles within the public sector.
- For example, it is legitimate for an expectation that public sector workers facing applicants everyday should appear neutral and not be affiliated with any religion, so that there is no danger of the applicants thinking that the public sector worker is biased towards or against a certain religion.

Counter-point

- The ban is discriminatory as it can never be justified to impose a restriction that heavily impacts a specific religion.
- Many Muslim women will not be able to change their convictions and not wear their headscarves just because they have to work in the public sector as the headscarf forms an integral part of their culture and identity, and in many cases they will feel insecure and vulnerable without the headscarf.
- Such a ban is discriminatory towards a particular religion and should not be allowed.

END OF PAPER

Final Advice

Arrive well rested, well fed and well hydrated

The LNAT is an intensive test, so make sure you're ready for it. Ensure you get a good night's sleep before the exam (there is little point cramming) and don't miss breakfast. If you're taking water into the exam then make sure you've been to the toilet before so you don't have to leave during the exam. Make sure you're well rested and fed in order to be at your best!

Move on

If you're struggling, move on. Every question has equal weighting and there is no negative marking. In the time it takes to answer on hard question, you could gain three times the marks by answering the easier ones.

Afterword

Remember that the route to a high score is your approach and practice. Don't fall into the trap that "*you can't prepare for the LNAT*"– this could not be further from the truth. With knowledge of the test, some useful time-saving techniques and plenty of practice you can dramatically boost your score.

Work hard, never give up and do yourself justice.

Good luck!

About Us

Infinity Books is the publishing division of *Infinity Education Ltd.* We currently publish over 85 titles across a range of subject areas – covering specialised admissions tests, examination techniques, personal statement guides, plus everything else you need to improve your chances of getting on to competitive courses such as medicine and law, as well as into universities such as Oxford and Cambridge.

Outside of publishing we also operate a highly successful tuition division, called UniAdmissions. This company was founded in 2013 by Dr Rohan Agarwal and Dr David Salt, both Cambridge Medical graduates with several years of tutoring experience. Since then, every year, hundreds of applicants and schools work with us on our programmes. Through the programmes we offer, we deliver expert tuition, exclusive course places, online courses, best-selling textbooks and much more.

With a team of over 1,000 Oxbridge tutors and a proven track record, UniAdmissions have quickly become the UK's number one admissions company.

Visit and engage with us at:
Website (Infinity Books): www.infinitybooks.co.uk
Website (UniAdmissions): www.uniadmissions.co.uk
Facebook: www.facebook.com/uniadmissionsuk
Twitter: @infinitybooks7

Made in United States
Orlando, FL
04 November 2026

90201375R00087